Our Lent

Things We Carry

2nd edition

David Crumm

Read The Spirit Books

an imprint of
David Crumm Media, LLC
Canton, Michigan

For more information and further discussion, visit

http://www.OurLent.com

Cover art and design by
Rick Nease
www.RickNeaseArt.com

Published By
Read The Spirit Books
an imprint of
David Crumm Media, LLC
42015 Ford Rd., Suite 234
Canton, Michigan, USA

For information about customized editions, bulk purchases or permissions, contact David Crumm Media, LLC at info@David-CrummMedia.com

Contents

Dedication

To my lifelong companion on the sacred journey, Amy.

Preface

OBSERVANCE OF LENT IS booming across the U.S., especially among non-traditional groups including many evangelical and emergent churches. Even Catholic parishes nationwide are seeing a rise in season-long observances. This makes sense in an era of turbulent change in our world. A return to spiritual practices—from praying daily to following the centuries-old traditions of Lent—is a journey that reconnects us with the timeless wisdom of our faith. *grounds + centers forms foundation*

This sacred season recalls the heart of the Gospels that 2 billion Christians around the world regard as a sacred guide to *something that doesn't* living, so the diversity of our Lenten experience may seem surprising. Eastern and Western Christians sometimes converge on the same Lenten calendar; sometimes they are weeks apart, due to differences in calculating the date of Easter each year. Western Christians, those from the branches of the Christian tree that grew from Rome and branched out through the Reformation, count Lent's 40 days as starting with Ash Wednesday but *to Maundy Ram?*

excluding Sundays. Eastern Christians, those generally called Orthodox, start their 40 days on a Monday, counting Sundays, but excluding the week leading up to Easter.

Some Christians fast; some don't. Millions of Western Christians retain a custom of limited fasting; millions of Eastern Christians follow a far more ambitious set of fasting traditions. Many Christians prayerfully make significant sacrifices during this season, while others have barely acknowledged the season throughout most of their lives.

So, why is this season rising in popularity? As a careful observer of religious life over the past three decades, I believe that Lent is the perfect Christian season for this 21st century era of change, anxiety and spiritual transformation. Uncluttered by the commercial avalanche that has all but buried the Advent season that leads to Christmas, Lent retains much of its ancient religious potential. That's why Mel Gibson struck such a huge cultural nerve with his controversial film, *The Passion of the Christ*.

University of Michigan sociologist Dr. Wayne E. Baker, in his landmark study "America's Crisis of Values: Reality and Perception," used the massive global waves of data from the World Values Survey to demonstrate the unusual nature of American religious values. Compared with other global cultures, Baker showed that Americans are unique: We are so overwhelmingly religious that we resemble countries like Iran in our spiritual intensity. But, when it comes to values concerning self-expression, Americans surpass Scandinavians in our zeal. We are people of deep faith coupled with an equally deep desire to freely share our religious experiences.

In such an era, Lent is the perfect, untarnished blend of religious tradition and spiritual adventure—ancient roots still blossoming in self-reflection and self-expression. Or, to put it another way, Lent is the *Lord of the Rings* of scriptural stories—a loyal fellowship of men and women fearlessly summoning all of their traditional knowledge as they make their way toward a dangerous encounter in a city where the fate of the world hangs in the balance. Yet, unlike J.R.R. Tolkien's trilogy, each of us is invited to make our own Lenten pilgrimage each year. That's how millions of Christians experience the season—preparing their hearts, minds and daily lives in fresh ways for this epic quest. Thousands of churches now distribute devotional books to help shape the Lenten journey. The core of this season is a life-changing, personal and communal encounter with the sacred.

Now, many religious leaders are aware of Lent's rising popularity and are hoping to make fresh connections among this vast array of scattered pilgrims. In this *Our Lent* devotional book—and online materials available at: http://www.OurLent.info—we are providing 40 days of reflections, connecting things in the Gospels' climactic journey of Jesus with things we carry in our own lives today. The big picture behind *Our Lent* is this: Jesus' journey 2,000 years ago was a public pilgrimage of such profound importance that we mark it each year, day by day, even in the opening of the third millennium since Jesus walked the Earth. Rather than leaving such a powerful religious narrative locked inside individual churches and individual lives—we are moving the Lenten adventure back into the biggest public roadway of our time: the creatively flexible digital world. For example, we invite you to visit us online to learn more about opportunities to order quantities of this book with the possibility of personalizing a "group read" for your congregation by putting your church's logo on the cover of the copies you order. You can even add your own introductory pages to this book for your church or organization. Plus, you can enjoy *Our Lent* on any digital reader you carry, including a Kindle, Nook, iPad or iPhone. *Our Lent* materials also will be added throughout the season to our website. This *Our Lent* experience now is as adaptable and portable as the original journey 2,000 years ago.

Some of the things we will encounter in these 40 days are spiritual ideas that Jesus conveyed to his followers, for example: In the second chapter of our journey, which draws from Matthew 20:29-34, we join Jesus in encountering two blind men—and an even more profound blindness in the crowd surrounding this pair. It's a brief but fascinating encounter in the Gospels and reflects on how we, as Christians today, disregard the marginalized along our own highways. While some things along this journey are scenes and lessons, most of the things in our 40-chapter journey are quite tangible things: coins, basins, bowls, bread, cups, swords and tables, to name a few. This was the stuff of Jesus' world. It's still the stuff of our lives, 2,000 years after Jesus' world-shaking walk to Jerusalem.

This year, come along. Walk with us.

Invite a friend to accompany you.

You're already carrying things.

Help us to lighten the load.

—*David Crumm, Founding Editor, ReadTheSpirit.com*

Ash Wednesday: Hitting the Lenten Road Together

A YOUNG NEW ORLEANS husband and wife, while reluctantly packing up their U-Haul truck, were captured in a color photograph for a front-page New York Times report about the failures faced by many New Orleans urban pioneers. The bitter twist in that Times story was that many of those brave pioneers, like the couple with the U-Haul, had thought that they were committed to returning and rebuilding the city after the Katrina floods—but the folks in the story had discovered that The Big Easy was a far tougher place to live post-Katrina than they ever imagined. We won't name that New Orleans couple, partly to mercifully let their memory fade as they rumble off toward some new hope for home—but partly because it doesn't matter who they were.

In a profound way, they are all of us. They're a striking icon at the start of our Lenten journey.

More and more, as Americans, we are rootless. Sometimes, we're driven by storms like Hurricane Katrina in 2005. But, more often we're like that couple with the U-Haul—driven not by a storm itself but by the needs of our families, the fortunes of our employers and the fears and hopes that swell in our hearts as much as in our heads.

If you doubt this simple truth, consider the speed with which cremation rates are rising nationwide. This may sound like a rather morbid detour in our Lenten journey, but consider these data for just a moment: This year, 1 in 3 of us who pass away will not be taking a traditional drive to a family plot. When we go, an ever-increasing number of us are expecting to be turned into far-more-portable ash. And, in some areas of the West Coast and Florida, 2 out of 3 of us who pass away this year already have chosen cremation. Some of us are choosing this option because it's cheaper, but the data show that it's largely because millions of us are rootless—most of us simply don't envision a hometown anymore where we expect to be planted conveniently near the homes of descendants who will visit occasionally to place flowers and flags.

Our iconic images of home are transforming. Norman Rockwell's beloved image of Thanksgiving dinner featuring a golden turkey triumphantly presented at the family homestead showed up with a gut-wrenching twist in the movie *American Gangster*. The family gathered for that movie banquet was a clan of predators, preying on the rest of us. And, that film was based on a true story—a truly somber note, isn't it?

But, here's the timeless note of hope: We can face even the bitterest truths, because fundamentally we are heading down the Lenten road as a People of Good News. We know our destination. In the turbulent oceans of change all around us these days, we are the people who know how to swim, to sail—and to pull others into the boats with us.

More than that, on his own Earth-shaking journey to Jerusalem 2,000 years ago, Jesus tried his best to equip us for the road. He kept picking up and pointing out things along the way that he wanted us all to remember—like programming the Gospel equivalent of a spiritual GPS. Perhaps if he drove to Jerusalem today in a tour bus with his friends, Jesus would tap all of his lessons into a hand-held device, post them to the online Cloud—and we'd never get lost again.

The Good News is we're *not* lost. Maybe restless, rootless and bruised, but we're not lost. More than 2 billion Christians around the world are marking the Lenten season in some fashion this year, including hundreds of millions of Americans. All around the world, we are people on the move. We're just like Jesus' friends two millennia ago. And, the truth of this journey is so timeless that it is echoed and reflected everywhere we look—if we only have eyes and ears to truly recognize the meaningful things along our path.

Do you know the most frequently asked question by news reporters covering refugee stories in Africa and Asia, today? This same question pops up all around the world, when reporters talk to men, women and children who were burned out, bombed out, blown out, driven out. Can you think of the question? It's this: "What did you carry with you when you left your home?"

What would *you* carry?

It's not an idle question because, whether you know it or not, we're all moving in our rapidly transforming global culture. That young couple in New Orleans rumbling down the road in a nearly overloaded U-Haul—that's us—our human family.

We're already carrying things as we search for home.

Things We Ignore Along the Way May Haunt Us

ON THIS LENTEN JOURNEY, we only need to open our eyes and ears to discover Jesus' lessons resonating all around us. That's because our spiritual journey is both timeless and true. Each day in our 40-day journey, we will recall things from Jesus' journey toward Jerusalem—and beyond. But, beware! Sometimes this journey is so painfully true that our hearts ache when fresh light falls on our past.

On one level, there's nothing new here. These things have been sitting there in the Gospels for thousands of years. On another level, we're following Jesus' timeless call to see the world in new ways—so most of these things continue to echo in surprisingly urgent ways from headlines around the world.

Today, we start with one of Jesus' powerful demonstrations of the importance of sight in this final journey of his life. Today's reflection centers on a small incident—a matter so seemingly insignificant that people wanted to overlook what was happening in Jesus' day, too. The incident unfolded just outside the town of Jericho as Jesus and his followers were taking the road up to Jerusalem.

For Jesus' followers, it was a fresh warning that—in the process of choosing what to carry and what to shed as we lighten our load for this journey—our spiritual lives depend upon not shedding the wrong things. That's especially true if we even think about shedding our concern for people who desperately need our help.

Like all things in this 40-day journey, this lesson is as old as the Gospels and as fresh as news reports from around the world.

Most Americans know about Anne Frank, the iconic image of the Holocaust's tragic cost in human life. Just before founding *ReadTheSpirit* in 2007, I was a religion newswriter for a major newspaper chain—and I was jolted along with the rest of the world, early that year, when long-lost letters resurfaced from Anne's father, Otto Frank. More than 60 years after World War II, this startling news broke from a Jewish archive in New York City. As it turns out, these letters had been overlooked all those years in a sea of Holocaust-era files.

Once uncovered, though, the news of these letters echoed around the world. Perhaps it is a sign of how deeply ambivalent we feel in the United States about admitting our own wartime culpability, but this news did not echo across American media as strongly as it hit newspapers in Europe and Asia.

The Times of London headlined the story:

"Anne Frank's Doomed American Dream—Father's Letters Reveal Bid for Visa."

That was a fairly muted headline, among the newspapers hitting the streets that day in London. *The Daily Telegraph's* blunt headline proclaimed:

" 'Anti-Semitic' America Closed Its Doors to Family of Anne Frank."

And there it was—a long-buried sin unearthed in the roadway for all to see, after all these years. We have always known that it was the Nazi genocide of Jews that ultimately killed Anne Frank, after she was discovered along with her family in an attic and was sent to a concentration camp. But, now, we've learned that, as Americans, we can't sigh sadly at the end of Anne's diary and say to ourselves: "Well, no one could have saved them." The truth is: We could have, as Americans.

That's a harsh judgment for Americans to accept, but virtually all of the research by Holocaust scholars hammers home this point. Even the existing immigration quotas at the time—quotas that could have saved many Jewish families—were left unfilled by U.S. officials. Historians have traced this refusal to shelter fleeing families to attitudes among a number of key figures in Washington, D.C. who seem scandalously callous by today's standards.

Our own U.S. Holocaust Memorial Museum in Washington, D.C. documents this terrible truth. There were anti-Semitic figures in our government, but America's cold shoulder to these refugees wasn't the result of a secret cabal of powerful men. This was a widespread American attitude at the time.

The attitude was as public as the hugely popular, nationwide radio broadcasts of the Rev. Charles Coughlin, who rebuked anyone who dared to *cry out* on behalf of the plight of Jews in Europe and sternly ordered them to be quiet.

What does this have to do with the start of our Lenten journey? In a word: **everything**. If you're Christian, do those phrases emphasized above echo from the Gospels? Perhaps you don't recall this passage in Matthew, Mark and Luke. It's a brief scene in which Jesus is making his way toward Jerusalem for the Passover observance and passes through the ancient city of Jericho. Here's how Matthew tells the story in 20:29–34: (It's also in Mark 10:46–52 and Luke 18:35–43.)

> As they left Jericho, a crowd followed. At the side
> of the road sat two blind men. When they real-
> ized that Jesus was passing by, they cried out,
> "Have mercy on us, O Lord, son of David!"
> The crowd rebuked them and sternly ordered
> them to be quiet. Instead, the blind men cried all
> the louder.
> Jesus stood still. Then, he called to the men, ask-
> ing, "What will you have me do for you?"

They said, "Lord, open our eyes."
Jesus had compassion on them and touched their
eyes. And immediately they received sight—and
followed him.

This may sound like other healing passages in the Gospels.
We've all heard these stories preached from Christian pulpits.
Usually, the emphasis in the preaching is on the great faith of the
people asking Jesus for help—and the miraculous nature of Jesus'
response. But, this story is intriguing because the exact identity of
the blind men outside Jericho didn't seem to matter to the Gospel
writers. The more we think about this story, we see that, in fact, it's
not a story about an individual person's persistence as much as it
is a stunning rebuke by the crowd as the young rabbi makes his
way to Passover!

The two hinges of this story are: first, the crowd's attempt to
silence the blind men's pleas; then, the second hinge is the dramatic three-word sentence: "Jesus stood still." Thinking about that
ancient story, with the contemporary truth of the Otto Frank letters as a backdrop, doesn't the hair stand up on the back of your
neck as you think about Jesus' response?

As we hit the road for Lent, let's first stop like Jesus and look
around us for the many people crying out for help. As we shed our
burdens to lighten our spiritual load, let's be careful that we don't
shed our concern for those in need.

After all, the young rabbi was a man on a mission. Christians
say it was the greatest mission in the history of the world. And
yet, when confronted with these pleas from the desperate outcasts
near Jericho, the young rabbi ignored the powerful voices yelling
at him.

Instead, Jesus stood still.

He was moved by compassion.

And soon, others were moving with him.

A Reckless Woman and a Jar of Precious Oil

OH, TO HAVE JUST one Gospel in our Bible written by a woman! There are portions of Jesus' journey that are so difficult for us to see through the mists of two millennia and the masculine filters of the four Gospel writers who made it into the final sacred text.

What would a Margaret Atwood have done with today's scene? Along the road to Jerusalem, Jesus and his male friends encounter the embarrassing, sensual extravagance of an out-of-control woman who carries a jar of expensive, perfumed oil into their inner circle and pours it out onto Jesus.

Matthew, Mark and John all set the scene late in their narratives within the final sequence of Jesus' drama (Mark's version is at 14:3-9). As fairly pragmatic narrators, these three cast the scene to foreshadow Jesus' death and resurrection. Surely, since this scene appears in all four Gospels, this was a well-known incident in this young rabbi's life. Perhaps it happened more than once to him and was such an infamous kind of scene that any self-respecting writer had to deal with it in some way. They all had to tuck the scene away safely in the narrative to have its shocking impact muted by a more important purpose in the overall story.

But, even in those three accounts, one point is clear: Jesus' disciples had trailed their rabbi up hill and down, through countless sermons and late-night chats—and yet these 12 guys apparently didn't have a clue how Jesus saw the people he encountered on their journey.

They had little excuse! They had been blessed themselves by this rabbi's compassionate vision. Jesus had recognized them as invaluable, unique and precious people—and, yet, the disciples only saw the object that this woman carried. They missed that there was also an invaluable, unique and precious person behind the jar of oil.

Perhaps Luke (7:36-50) was the only Gospel writer who truly got the anointing scene right. It's only in Luke that we see the full drama of the scene—set much earlier in Jesus' ministry. Luke's placement of the scene early on explains a lot. Perhaps that's why the disciples failed to recognize and evaluate this visitor in Jesus' own compassionate style—because, in Luke, the encounter happens so early in their time with him. The followers were still hopeless newcomers to the community that Jesus was creating.

Luke by far is the best sculptor of this scene. Only here do we have the full-blown description of the woman anointing Jesus not only with her jar of oil but also with her tears as she weeps over his feet—and dries his feet with her long hair. The overwhelming, heartbreaking nature of her response to him is inescapable in Luke. If Luke had set this scene later in his Gospel, in the context of Jesus' tragic demise, the emotional and physical magnitude of this scene would have been so over the top that we could barely stand to read it, I suspect.

To what can we compare such a thing as this anointing, 2,000 years later?

Well, to supplement your Lenten reading, consider an amazing book by Jeffrey A. Kottler, chair of the Department of Counseling at California State University, called *Divine Madness: Ten Stories of Creative Struggle*. Imagine reading Luke 7 in parallel with Kottler's chapter, "Judy Garland: Under the Rainbow."

Kottler describes Garland's life and her enduring appeal as a shooting star. On one level, she was an enormous talent who glistened in Hollywood's firmament in song, dance and theatrical performances that rank among the greatest moments ever captured on film. But, on another level, as has been documented in many biographical sketches of Garland, she was an abused young woman who went on to abuse herself with various substances until her star eventually imploded.

She was "wild, impulsive, uninhibited, reckless," Kottler says. These were precisely the qualities that mesmerize millions of fans to this day. Even the talented young singers and dancers in the hit TV series *Glee* produced an extended homage to Judy Garland to close out their 2011 season. The power of Judy Garland's persona is the blending, within a single person, of transcendent hopes of rainbows and the tragedy of broken dreams.

Unfortunately, in Jesus' journey, his followers entirely missed the real person behind the precious oil. All they saw was the expensive thing the woman carried into their midst: the opulence of the perfume.

As usual, Jesus saw something much different, much larger. And, Luke may be the only Gospel writer who truly captures the hope in Jesus' response. In the face of harsh criticism, Jesus defends the woman, recognizing the immense love welling up in her heart. He realizes that she has led a deeply troubled life. And he parts with these words to her: "Your faith has saved you. Go in peace."

That may be why, in Luke's Gospel, skipping into Chapter 8, we suddenly find that not only are men following Jesus along his challenging journey—but a whole host of women are following, now, as well!

Our Most Controversial Story Reveals a Cat in the Hat

HOW DO YOU SEE Jesus? Christians affirm he was fully God and fully human. But, *what was he like?* How did that human personality play out day by day? Today's story probes that question and—since *ReadTheSpirit* began reflecting on Lent in 2008—this story has been our most controversial among the 40. See what you think. Maybe we've got this story all wrong? But, *maybe—* maybe our story today will deepen your contemplation on scenes so iconic that they are frozen forever in canvas, fresco, bronze and stained glass.

One reason today's story gets little reflection is its placement in congregations around the world. It's a shame that the rigidly-minded creators of the Common Lectionary wasted the story of Jesus' entry into Jerusalem in Luke 19 by delaying it for a public reading in churches on Palm Sunday—and presenting this complex drama of Jesus' entry in a single swath. This is one of the richest scenes in the entire Lenten journey and, when this story is read on Palm Sunday each year, the best details get buried in palm fronds and the anxious anticipation of the holiday approaching in seven days.

So, let's spend a little time examining the choicest details in this narrative, shall we? Since our Lenten journey focuses on tangible things that appear in this most famous of all dramas, then let's start with the young animal that was "borrowed" by Jesus' disciples as his provocative mode of transportation into the Holy City.

Yes, we know that this detail of a "colt" that Jesus rides is designed to echo the royal entry described in Zechariah 9:9. But that's such a Paint-by-Numbers reading of the scene. Think about the larger drama here and the cleverness of this rebellious young rabbi who was barely out of his 20s and wasn't above poking his fingers in authorities' eyes from time to time.

Can you envision the prologue to this scene? Jesus and his followers are heading toward Jerusalem and Jesus is anxious about what's ahead of him. His temper is rising, frankly, because he's weary of the way the authorities have tried, at every turn, to trap him. Plus, he's already wrestling with the extremely tough decisions looming ahead of him. People aren't listening. They don't get what he's trying to proclaim. His emotions are spilling over! It's in these days, as Jesus contemplates what lies ahead that John's Gospel records the Bible's shortest verse: "Jesus wept."

But, hold on a moment! Jesus is—well, he's *Jesus*, which means he keeps his cool and his good humor. As our scene opens, it's a sunny day around Jerusalem and Jesus makes a playfully provocative decision: "Go get me a colt, even though that's sure to annoy some folks. Hey, do it anyway and let's see what happens." No, that dialogue isn't in the Bible. But we're just envisioning the scene, filling in more details than we find in the classic paintings and stained-glass windows. Maybe Jesus talked to his followers like that?

If we believe that the Gospels aren't merely an accounting of moves in a cosmic chess match ... If we believe that the narratives are rooted in real details in Jesus' life ... And, if we truly believe, as Christians, that he was as much human as he was divine, then can't we picture this very savvy young rabbi looking at the colorful crowds approaching the giant gates, the sunlight playing on the golden walls of the city. Perhaps Jesus actually cracked a grin that day as he sent his friends off to snatch the colt for him.

Is this an uncomfortable way to approach the sacred text? Perhaps. But, then, the gift that Dr. Seuss gave to American baby boomers on March 1, 1957, was a deliberate finger-in-the-eye to those stodgy, pedestrian, old narratives about Dick, Jane, Sally and Spot. In fact, that's why he chose the name Sally for the young girl in *The Cat in the Hat*. This was Sally's true, literary coming-out party!

In *The Annotated Cat*, literary scholar Philip Nel says that Seuss deliberately intended to set children's imaginations free. In a 1960s interview, Seuss himself said that he wanted to move beyond the "old dull stuff" in the Dick and Jane primers. Despite recent nostalgia among baby boomers for those Technicolor-style Dick and Jane illustrations—let's face it: They were incredibly dull stories. In toppling their well-established literary tower, Seuss succeeded beyond his wildest dreams. Perhaps, in Jerusalem that day, Jesus succeeded beyond his followers' dreams as they saw the palms waving. They'd certainly had a ball snatching the colt for him! Can't you imagine them? As Jesus was settling himself on the animal's back, they probably were jostling each other playfully, asking, "Did you hear that guy shouting at us when we grabbed the colt?" And, "Wow, he was steamed at what we pulled back there! Pretty exciting, huh?"

Jesus was shaking his head, grinning affectionately at these guys. The women in the group were shaking their heads, too. Those goofy guys were horsing around, again—and at such a serious time!

Now, this is the point in the story that's so controversial. Most Christians recall only the paintings and stained glass. They read the original story as describing an animal carefully pre-arranged. Jesus and his disciples certainly never "snatched" it! But think about the tumult in Jerusalem at that moment. If you've ever worked with animals, you know the earthy and unpredictable nature of the scene. And, whether the colt was patiently waiting—or was grabbed in the mist of jostling good humor—there's no question that Jesus was embodying something provocative that day. Jesus was showing the crowd—and especially the Romans—that their world was spiraling out of their control.

If you dare to envision the scene this way, you're not alone. Best-selling Christian teachers from the evangelical John Eldredge to the provocative Bible scholar John Dominic Crossan have published recent books urging Christians to recapture Jesus' "in-your-face" challenge to authorities. It was Jesus' deliberate finger-in-the-eye of Rome that provoked his execution, Crossan writes. And Eldredge sums up Jesus in two words: Beautiful Outlaw.

Uncomfortable now? Well, remember good ol' Dr. Seuss for a moment. Seuss was a master at letting events spiral further and further out of control until everything seemed hilariously head over heels. But, Seuss always conveyed a confident assumption that, somehow, everything would work out in the end. In the final pages, the Cat in the Hat would unleash a clean-up crew. The world would turn 'round right. And, that's what lies ahead of us in the Lenten journey, isn't it? The whole cosmos turning 'round right?

Is it blasphemous to read the Gospels in parallel with Dr. Seuss? Or is it a way to explore deeper, timeless meanings in the things that were carried in this ancient journey?

First Monday of Lent and Even the Stones Cry Out!

YES, STONES. THEY'RE THINGS in our Lenten journey that are so easy to miss in the hustle and bustle of our daily lives. Properly speaking, they aren't even things to see along the road—they are the road itself!

Noticing stones, let alone hearing them speak to us, is like pausing in the Louvre to contemplate the frame around a masterpiece. Or, perhaps it's like creeping up to the foot of the stage during a play and peering behind the curtains at the vast expanse of rigging surrounding the main drama. Who would do that? An usher would kick us out on our ears.

Yet, this is one of the two remaining things in what is often called Jesus' "Triumphal Entry into Jerusalem" that we'll consider before we get to the Climax of Act I. Of course, the Bible is divided into chapters, now, but if we envision this particular Lenten story as a great drama, then Act I takes us from the wildness of the anointing at Bethany and the boisterous entry into Jerusalem to the looming explosion at the Temple in Jerusalem that would seal Jesus' fate—and bring down the curtain on this opening act.

In the midst of such high drama, who can fault most of the Gospel writers for entirely missing this detail we are examining today? These speaking stones are such a cryptic part of this drama that they can be found in only a single Gospel. However, they're certainly not superfluous scenery. They're among the most startling "things" in this journey. You won't find them in John, where Jesus has no immediate lines at the close of the big entry scene. John jumps quickly to another scene in which the young rabbi is talking with his friends about the metaphor of seeds buried in the Earth. Or, how about Matthew? Well, he's in such a rush to get to the key scene at the Temple that Matthew overlooks the stones completely.

And, what should we expect from Mark—the brief "CliffsNotes Gospel"? Mark jump-cuts from the entry—without including any of Jesus' lines in the closing of that scene—to the very next day when we do get one other hint of the ominously rising level of discontent. That's the scene in Mark in which the disciples start gossiping about having spotted Jesus cursing a barren fig tree. Not only was Jesus so uncharacteristically grouchy that he actually began cussing out a tree—but, worse yet, as Mark puts it: "His disciples heard it!"

It's Luke's eloquence that includes the stones, followed by Jesus' tears. It's a startling, multifaceted scene in Luke. Here is a brilliant writer, unafraid to open up the drama on a scale that surpasses even grand opera. We're talking about a scene in which the very seams of the world are coming unraveled. The stones of the roadway are about to cry out—and this wise rabbi, who some around Jerusalem are saying is divine and who was supremely confident just a moment ago with that wacky woman in Bethany, now is reduced to tears at the mere sight of the Holy City.

Here's how Luke describes the stones:

> Some of the Pharisees in the multitude said,
> "Master, tell your disciples to quiet down!"
> And Jesus answered: "I tell you, if these people
> held their peace, the stones would cry out!"

A gasp is appropriate from the audience right there. This is a transcendent moment, when Christians glimpse God and Man

---

struggling mightily within Jesus in these final days of his life on Earth. This is the kind of electrically charged moment felt by people who have survived a heart attack or attended the funeral of a spouse, a parent or a sibling—someone very close to us. It's the sensation that leads us to utter words like, "I'm suddenly more aware than I've ever been before that life itself is so beautiful and precious!" It's as though, for an instant, we lift our eyes above "the glass darkly" through which St. Paul tells us we usually view the world—and glimpse with full force the potency of God's Creation—even the stones beneath our feet.

Who in our world today routinely focuses on the stones ahead? In recent years, Andrew Carroll has become one of America's leading experts on wartime correspondence. His *Grace Under Fire: Letters of Faith in Times of War* is a collection of letters from the American Revolution to the War in Iraq that involve spirituality. One thing readers discover instantly in Carroll's book is that war zones heighten human awareness to the point that many people are driven into electrically charged moments.

From 2003, Carroll includes an email that NBC News Correspondent David Bloom sent home to his wife Melanie just one day before he died of a blood clot, caused by too many long hours cramped inside a military vehicle with his knees pressed to his chest. In his note home on the eve of the looming tragedy, Bloom clearly was a man passing through the hyper-awareness of a transcendent moment. In David's final email home to Melanie, he said that God was carrying him to unfathomable depths of reflection.

So it was 2,000 years ago on the rocky streets of Jerusalem, where the hinges of history were opening and even the rocks in the road were about to cry out!

Layers in Palms— and Onions, Too

HEY! WHERE ARE YOU?

We're just starting this Lenten journey—and we can barely see each other today! It's hard to see past all these waving palm fronds! Come on! We're over here! Right here, in the midst of Act I in our timeless journey. Better huddle up, because just around the corner in our story there is going to be a big, dangerous boom in the Temple precincts—then a falling curtain.

Today, we're still standing in that enormous, jostling crowd in the streets of Jerusalem. Yes, that's us, beneath the layers of waving palm fronds! Or, as Steve Spreitzer, a nationally known coordinator of diversity programs, likes to put it: Perhaps, we're standing within the spiritual layers of an onion.

An onion? Steve is a playful guy. Among other things, he once organized an interfaith running club in the suburbs west of Detroit that mingled prayer, reflection, physical training and playful competitiveness. He called this group F5, which stands for Fun, Fitness, Family, Friendship and Faith. When Steve got wind of preparation for the *Our Lent* project, he wrote an email suggesting that we include an onion in our series of reflections.

Try as I might, scouring every Gospel translation I could find—I missed any reference to onions. Then, Steve alerted me that he was referring to the far-more-modern epistles of the monk Thomas Merton. So, I spent a couple of days scouring Merton's books—and this turned up a helpful revelation. Merton actually sounds like he is echoing a centuries-old aphorism about layers of an onion, attributed to Yiddish sources which goes like this:

Life is like an onion.
Why is life like an onion? Because you peel away layer after layer and when you come to the end you have nothing.

Here is the onion-like metaphor that Merton used in his 1961 book, *New Seeds of Contemplation*: Merton described the universal need for spiritual formation in our lives and argued that, without such a foundation, it is futile to try to wrap random layers of meaning around the hollow core of our lives. The greater our obsession with this problem of spiritual emptiness, Merton argued, the greater will be our obsession with enfolding our lives in seemingly colorful layers. He concluded that the problem with all of this anxious layering is that there may be nothing left at all in our lives if the layers are suddenly pulled away.

That's pretty grim stuff, especially on a sunny day in the streets of Jerusalem on which we're watching the green, emerald, golden, green, emerald, green colors flow as the palm fronds wave all around us.

In recent years, Steve Spreitzer tried to see past these many distracting layers by combining his Lenten journey with a rigorous Muslim approach to such a reflective season. For 40 days, Steve fasted from sunrise to sunset as Muslims do each year during the month of Ramadan. In a Muslim-style fast, a person gives up all food and drink, even water during daylight hours. Steve wanted to jump from his place in the spiritual drama to someone else's vantage point. Here's how Steve described the experience in an email:

"I experimented with what I called Rama-Lent. I applied the prescriptions given to Muslims during Ramadan, which call for no eating, drinking or sexual activity between sunup and sundown. As you might imagine, this was brutal, especially considering my ignoring the critically important communitarian aspect of Ramadan. During this holy month, Muslims pray together early in the morning, eat a full meal together, pray several more times during the day, offering each other encouragement and then coming together to break their fast and to pray once more. I would like to say I had my best Lent ever last year, but you would have to ask my wife, my family and my co-workers for the real skinny.

"I did find myself having more time to pray and reflect once I got past the initial hunger and gained some control over the typical use of food in my life to quiet my fears or to keep my belly full. I also came to realize my utter dependence on God's grace and seemed to seek God more in every aspect of my life. Finally, I came face to face with just how broken and vulnerable I was."

Yes! That's the same point we're sharing with you today. We're asking where you are in our little band of travelers. Are you lost in the palm fronds?

Are you starting to contemplate all the layers surrounding us? Are you peering through those palm fronds? Are you peeling away the layers of the onion?

Confronting Coins, Cash, Capital and ... Coffee

NOW, IN OUR LENTEN journey, we come to things we all carry: Coins, Cash, Dole, Lucre, Moolah, Riches, Treasure, Wealth and Green! Shocked to find so much money talk in the Gospels? Since the 1980s, a central mantra of the red-hot seeker-church marketing movement has been: People hate churches that talk about money.

Now that the seeker model is in eclipse, the error of that anti-money assumption is obvious. These days, hot, young evangelists tend to ask for bigger levels of commitment, not less. Perhaps the learning curve would have been shorter had the elders at any of the trend-setting seeker churches of the 1980s hired as their teaching pastor a young rabbi from Nazareth.

That young rabbi left us so few sermons (he was preaching, after all, before the age of YouTube) that we're frequently frustrated by the brevity of his remarks. For instance, the rabbi said precious little about divorce, except to condemn it, and we're still scratching our heads over those few comments he left us on that widespread practice.

Or, it's almost scandalous to consider how frequently he talked about slavery, yet neglected to leave us a pointed condemnation of that evil institution. So much of his fragmented record is frustrating to discern today!

But Coins, Cash, Dole, Lucre, Moolah, Riches, Treasure, Wealth and Green? Jesus was crystal clear on that subject! Most of his parables are rooted in one form of commerce or another—from the greedy prodigal son to the sharp-eyed gentleman who emptied his 401(k) to purchase a beautiful pearl he discovered while visiting the country one day.

Money is everywhere in Jesus' teachings—from the robbers who nearly murder a man on the Jericho road to some of the most famous talks Jesus gave in the final days of his life. In many ways, this young rabbi would be better suited to a teaching chair in business ethics at a prominent university, than to most parish pulpits. And why? Because Jesus' entire teaching ministry can be summed up in one word: Connection.

Jesus' Greatest Commandment—still ahead of us in this journey—represents the entire Law and the Prophets artfully distilled into two simple rules of connection, or as Jesus puts it in Matthew 22:37–39:

> **Love the Lord your God with all your heart, all your soul and all your mind. This is the first and great commandment.**
> And the second is like it: **Love your neighbor as yourself.**

Do you see his perspective on commerce a little more clearly, now? Coins, Cash, Dole, Lucre, Moolah, Riches, Treasure, Wealth and Green are the most powerful, tangible, universal embodiments of connection that we carry with us. Of course, the wisest religious sages throughout history have recognized this truth. The Talmud, the crowning achievement of centuries of Jewish ethics and culture, is full of discussions of commerce. So are the teachings of the Prophet Muhammad. So are the writings of countless religious leaders, including the late Pope John Paul II, whose reflections were forged by his own painful odyssey from Fascism through Communism and into the postmodern world. In fact, some of John Paul's best messages were about the sacred meaning of human work and the sinful injustices of systems that oppress the poor.

So, quite naturally, the final scene in Act I of our Lenten drama involves commerce and connection. John is the only Gospel that sets this money scene very early in Jesus' years of ministry. The other Gospel writers vote 3-to-1 that Jesus' stormy confrontation with merchants in the Temple Religious Supply Stores came in the final days of his life. This makes sense on various levels. Many modern historians and Bible scholars agree that this very likely was the civil disturbance that sparked Jesus' eventual conviction by the Romans.

Given that entire context, especially Jesus' savvy awareness of commerce and his frequent reflections on the subject—then why on Earth was he upset enough to charge into the midst of the Temple's busy mini-mall and start toppling display cases? The answer is Jesus' clear-eyed vision of how commerce should work in a community and, as he busted his way through racks and shelving units, scattering the stock and outraging the Jerusalem Chamber of Commerce—he cried out phrases that his followers would have remembered instantly from—well, from long, long ago.

Jesus borrowed lines from the Prophet Isaiah's impassioned, idealistic call for a "house of prayer for all peoples." And, for good measure, Jesus threw in lines from the Prophet Jeremiah's dire warning that anyone who forgets God's most basic concern for strangers, orphans, widows and the vulnerable risks turning the Temple into "a den of thieves." And, like most of these things we are examining in our journey—this tale is not only true, it's timeless.

So, we'll close here by quoting the recently discovered "Lamentation of the Prophet Schultz." That's Howard Schultz, the visionary who joined the regional Starbucks Coffee firm in the U.S. Northwest in the early 1980s and transformed it into the world's fastest growing denomination of urban temples. *Business Week Online* summarized Schultz's shocking two-page memo, which unexpectedly cried out prophetically from the very heart of the vast

Starbucks empire. Basically, Schultz was decrying decisions his company had made during its massive expansion that fueled efficiency or helped cut costs at the expense of diminishing the aura and environment of Starbucks.

Schultz's entire memo is available many places online, but here's the key line. In exasperation, Schultz seemed to be verbally overturning the tables of his own empire, crying out that his beloved stores "no longer have the soul of the past."

Well, 2,000 years ago, a young rabbi from Nazareth approaches this same kind of prophetic task without so much as an Internet-enabled laptop. Nevertheless, Jesus' 22 key words would make it across the millennia to us:

> My house shall be called a house of prayer for all nations—but, you have made it a den of thieves.

And, the next thing we know, coins are flying everywhere!

As Tables Turn, is There Hope ... or Despair?

BEFORE WE LEAVE ACT I of our journey, there's one big question lingering. After contemplating the coins themselves yesterday, we finally are glimpsing the intellectual side of Jesus' violent protest in the Jerusalem Temple Supply Stores. Jesus was recalling a purer, older, prophetic vision of how community and connections are supposed to work. His shouts and his disruption that day were a plea for spiritual simplicity and social justice.

But, this was a rabbi as clever as a snake and as silver-tongued as a National Public Radio host. Why the violence in his protest? Why overturn tables? What was percolating in this young man's belly? What was exploding in his mind?

Well, it may help to step back from our journey for just a moment. You know, climb a hill. Take a long cool drink of water and look over our progress. Our journey is taking us from Act I into the balance of a four-act, five-table drama.

Where are five tables in this Lenten drama? Remember that, in an early scene, we paused around the table at Bethany for Jesus' anointing—and now we've come to this explosion of tables in the precincts of the Temple in Jerusalem. Perhaps you can glimpse the three tables on the horizon, but we won't spoil the surprises by squinting our eyes at them just yet.

That is, except to share a hint at what's to come from the vantage point of another traveler on another hilltop, writing to the Early Church about this drama. In his letter to the Colossians, this traveler described the central theme of the timeless journey as: "To reconcile all things." So if that was the goal, why the chaos, the violence, the flying coins, crashing display cases, tumbling tables?

For the Christians among us, who see the young rabbi as embodying both human and divine, perhaps this eruption is evidence of the cosmic struggle within him. A reconciliation may be looming, somewhere down this road. But the truth is that, after three years of knocking his head against the knotty old trunks of the olive trees, trying to preach as passionately as possible about the shape of God's kingdom, this young rabbi is coming to terms with the end of his journey.

For those of us who've sat through decades of liturgies, our eyes dimmed by the gilded frames around these iconic images, our ears dulled by thousands of sermons and homilies—it's hard to appreciate this explosive moment.

What contemporary life might echo such extreme poles of creative energy? In *Divine Madness: 10 Stories of Creative Struggle*, Jeffrey Kottler gives us a pretty convincing portrait of the hope and despair that raged within comic Lenny Bruce in the years before his 1966 death as a result of what Kottler describes as "pretty much being persecuted to death."

Of course, those of us who remember Bruce may consider it utter blasphemy to compare the young rabbi who died at 33 with the young comic who died at 41. But, we think there's value in the electric jolt of recalling Lenny Bruce at this point in our journey. The shocks in Jesus' messages have long since been muted and desensitized in our memories. But Bruce's raw material still has the potential to shock us. And, although Bruce's pathway led him to the depths of despair, recalling his moments of crisis just might illuminate these scenes of Jesus' crisis.

For example, think of the flying coins and Jesus' loud denunciations about "a den of thieves" in the Temple. We heard the same fury echoed in Lenny Bruce's: "We are living in a degenerate and debauched society!" He uttered this line in 1963 to a crowd in a club, toward the end of his career as he eyed uniformed policemen at the back of the room just itching to arrest him.

With a few adjustments for historical details, it could be a description of Jesus preaching in a city dangerously controlled by ruthless Roman authorities, ready to swoop down at any sign of unrest. Eventually, this would lead Bruce to a downward spiral of self-destruction, but at the pinnacle of this period, Kottler argues that Bruce began to focus his fury in intentional ways. What's amazing is that, in this explosive kind of situation, Bruce managed to pull off some of his greatest performances.

Again—with a few details changed—we could be describing the drama 2,000 years ago. So, with these memories of anger rising, tables overturning and a brilliant story unfolding all around us, we watch the curtain fall on Act I of our drama.

What lies ahead of us? Despair or hope? Perhaps both await us in the "things" we have yet to glimpse.

Trying to See the Tree, for the Forest

SOMETIMES WE CAN'T SEE the tree—for the forest of interpretation. That's why this Lenten journey, focused on the things
we carry, is such a refreshing approach to this all-too-worn route
of pilgrimage. And, there are *lots* of trees in this Lenten story! I
learned a lot about the power of trees through the work of an old
friend, Rabbi Daniel Syme, who became obsessed with visions
of trees in the Holy Land. In his 60s, Rabbi Syme marked out a
remarkable spiritual course for himself far beyond the walls of
his beloved Temple Beth El, Michigan's oldest Jewish congregation. For a year, Syme crisscrossed North America like a latter-day
Johnny Appleseed in his quest to raise money for the planting of
1 million trees in Israel—specifically in northern Israel where, in
his words, "Christian, Jewish and Muslim children all play." He
did this to replace trees destroyed by rocket fire from Lebanon.
This isn't a time or place to refight that war. It's enough to point
out that rabbis have been concerned about the foliage in the Holy
Land for thousands of years.

Today, we're on a spiritual pilgrimage, focusing on this puzzling image of a fig tree in Jesus' journey. In 21:18–19, Matthew
tells us:

"In the morning, as Jesus returned to Jerusalem, he was hungry. And, when he saw a fig tree nearby, he walked over to it. But, he found nothing on the tree, only leaves.

"Then he said to the tree: 'Let no fruit grow on you—ever!' And, that fig tree withered away."

Matthew goes on to interpret this odd little scene as an example of the power of prayer. But do we really buy that commentary? Aren't there far better examples of prayer's power throughout the Gospels? Do we need tips on organic gardening through prayer? We know from Bible scholars that the Gospel writers were not working from original transcripts of Jesus' sermons. These writers were not historians documenting each detail from Jesus' daily diary. They were sacred storytellers. With great reverence, they were artfully gathering the most important stories and teachings from Jesus' ministry and weaving them into their narratives of his life. In this case, it seems more likely that Matthew simply picked up excerpts of Jesus' wise words about the power of prayer from elsewhere in Jesus' ministry and edited them into the text at this point—as if they explained the fig tree scene.

But there's a timeless honesty in this story, we have to admit. Mark's version of the story sounds more like something that might actually happen on a long road trip among friends, doesn't it? Sometimes we get split up along the road, we look back and observe one another. And, one day as they approached Jerusalem, some of Jesus' followers were surprised to look over their shoulders and find their rabbi cussing out a fig tree. Perhaps you don't read that ancient story in this way, but one thing is clear: When you see a tree in Israel-Palestine, you feel drawn by a higher power to walk over and contemplate it!

I like the way Rabbi Syme puts it. He simply loves the beauty of trees—and the transcendent power of planting a tree—playing a role in the life of a creature that just might outlive us. Syme says he doesn't care if the people planting new trees in the Holy Land are Jewish or Christian, Muslim or Buddhist, atheist or mystic— he simply wants them to join him in planting trees.

Rabbi Syme recently said this: "Planting a tree is a religious act, a prayer if you will, a symbol of hope and a symbol of life and that's the kind of dimension that I want this program to have. Not just planting trees for the State of Israel, but a religious act that has some meaning to the individual and their rootedness in the Holy Land whether they're Christians, Muslims or Jews.

"You know, the story is told of a young man who comes across an older man planting a tree and he says, 'You'll never see it grow!'

"And the older man says, 'Just as my parents planted trees so that I would enjoy them, so I have the responsibility to plant trees for future generations.' To me, that's a metaphor for religious existence in our world. We should be planting seeds that someday, even after we are gone, will be left towering over our children and grandchildren."

Of course, as the young rabbi from Nazareth knew, as well, the ultimate vision of trees connects with our ultimate vision of God's creation. He would have known by heart the lines of Psalm 96:

> Let the Heavens rejoice, and the Earth be glad;
> Let the sea roar, and everything within its depths.
> Let the fields be joyful, and all that is within.
> Then shall all the trees of the wood rejoice before
> the Lord.

But is John Lennon in Heaven?

Everybody's talking and no one says a word ...
Strange days indeed!

—John Lennon

WELCOME TO ACT II in our drama! The fig tree scene, yester-day, was just a brief prelude to this phase of our journey, another reminder of this new kind of spiritual awareness we are exploring. And, just wait! In Act II, the young rabbi we're following takes this new mindfulness he has been cultivating in his followers and asks us to let that mindfulness blossom into an entirely new vision of the world around us.

Does that sound too esoteric? Well, Bible scholar Marcus Borg reminds us in his book, *Jesus: Uncovering the Life, Teachings, and Relevance of a Religious Revolutionary*, that Jesus' culture was based on a pragmatic view of not only the world, but of what it means to be a human in the world.

Jesus didn't see people as disconnected spheres—mind and body. He saw people as—well, people. We might call that a remarkably well-integrated view of humanity, but Jesus probably wouldn't have understood that remark. He probably would have responded: What is there to integrate? People are people. What we see, hear and feel from people is what those people truly are.

So, along the road today, the young rabbi pulls us aside for a brief moment and drops on us an amazing new tale that snaps our heads around to his whole new vision of the world. It's a short little story. Only Matthew even catches it and shares it with us in his Gospel. Entire books on this phase of Jesus' life overlook this little tale:

> A man had two sons. He came to the first, and
> said, "Son, go work today in my vineyard."
> This son answered, "I won't!" But, afterward, he
> repented and went to work.
> Then, the man came to his second son and said
> likewise to him.
> The second son answered, "I'll go, sir!" But, he
> never showed up for work.
> As Jesus finished the story, he asked: So which
> son did the will of his father?
> Jesus' followers said: "The first."
> And, Jesus said to them: "I say to you that tax
> collectors and harlots will go into the kingdom
> of God before you. For John [the Baptist] came
> to you, before me, calling for righteousness—
> and you didn't listen or follow. But the others,
> the tax collectors and harlots—they believed him
> and followed."

Wow! Sort of snaps our heads around, doesn't it? What Jesus is saying is that it doesn't matter how terrific we sound. What matters is how we live. The things we do actually matter to Jesus, not just what we may profess.

Jesus is talking about the same kind of disconnect that John Lennon observed in his haunting song about, "Strange Days," when he sang about watching everyone moving their mouths, yet not hearing a thing they were saying.

I've been amazed in recent years at how dramatically Lennon's legacy is being reinterpreted. At least two major documentaries, not to mention new biographies, have placed Lennon at a cross-roads in American culture. In an era long before U2, Lennon was the first pop superstar to throw his weight behind a global political movement, risking his career and even his life. Those of us who recall that era tended to regard Lennon's behavior, at the time, as a bizarre chapter in the disintegration of the Beatles.

But many persuasive voices now, including experts who appear in the film, *U.S. vs. John Lennon*, argue that Lennon's protests were brilliant performance art. In stunts like his famous "Bed-In" in Amsterdam and Montreal, Lennon manipulated his popularity to make a political point. At the height of the Vietnam War, he knew that paparazzi were dying to capture film and photos of a Beatles newlywed in bed with his wife, Yoko Ono.

The surprise was, as Lennon explains it in the new documentary: When the reporters finally were let into the bedroom—they found John and Yoko sitting there poised like angels in white. Not only that, they were angels talking and singing about a single theme: Peace.

Journalist, author and peace activist Tariq Ali appears in the film, among other observers, crediting Lennon as a major influence in the peace movement. Also in the documentary, Lennon explains that his goal was to become so single-minded in his pursuit of peace that people would snap their attention back from all the complex arguments about the war. Lennon says he wanted to make war and peace as clear-cut a choice as two products, side by side, on a grocery store shelf. At that point, Lennon says, all that would matter was the practical choice that each person would make.

Or as Jesus put it 2,000 years ago: The proof is pragmatic. Everything else in the story, Jesus tells us, is irrelevant noise. What matters is what we see a person actually doing!

John Lennon certainly skated along the far edges of culture and human behavior. He even urged us to imagine there is no heaven at all. But, perhaps, he really was urging his listeners to strip away all the distracting rhetoric, to clear away all the haze on our distant horizons—and to look clearly at the world, and at each other.

Painful Hatching of the Dixie Chicks

"HEY, LISTEN UP! LIFE is hard—and people can be incredibly cruel."

That might have been how Jesus prefaced his next parable. In Matthew, he sets up this parable with the one we explored yesterday—warning his followers that people pretty much are what they do. And, today, we're deeply inside this new pragmatic world in which Jesus is soberly advising his followers to look at the things of this world with a cold-eyed clarity. Clearly, this rabbi is on a thematic roll—and we get a parable that might be called "Murder in the Vineyard."

We most often hear this passage preached for its obvious foreshadowing of Jesus' crucifixion. That's almost certainly the reason that Matthew, Mark and Luke all place this story at precisely this point in their narratives. But, the foreshadowing theme is the obvious, nudge-your-ribs purpose of the parable. We know all about that. So, step back for a moment and look at this scene with the pragmatic eye that the young rabbi has been encouraging. What's going on here? Jesus certainly is starting to get very hard-headed in his advice to his followers. The story goes like this (we're recalling the version from Luke, because in Luke's Gospel Jesus tells the whole tale, right through the dismal conclusion):

> A certain man planted a vineyard, and leased it to tenants, then went into a far country for a long time. When it was harvest time, he sent a servant to these tenants to get his share from the vineyard, but the tenants beat the servant and sent him away empty.
>
> Again, the man sent a servant; and, again, they beat him and treated him shamefully, then sent him away empty.
>
> Again, he sent a third; they wounded him, too, and cast him out.
>
> Then, the lord of the vineyard asked: "What shall I do? I will send my beloved son; it may be that they will reverence him, when they see he is my son."
>
> But the tenants saw the son coming and they reasoned: "This is the heir! Let's kill him and the inheritance may be ours!" So, they cast him out of the vineyard and killed him.
>
> What, therefore, shall the lord of the vineyard do to them? He shall come and destroy these tenants and give the vineyard to others.

And when they heard this story, they said: "God forbid!"

Get that!?! The climax of this story, "Murder in the Vineyard," is the owner murdering the tenants. The King James Version uses the word "destroy," but contemporary versions, like the New International Version, put it even more bluntly and say "kill." It's a tragic cycle of violence in which the basest of human motives rule the day. Surely, that's dark pessimism talking. Is the world truly that cruel?

Remember the Dixie Chicks? The trio toured in 2010 with the Eagles and they occasionally perform with other top artists—but all three are mothers with kids and they've largely stepped back from the white-hot spotlight that nearly incinerated the trio in the years from 2003 to 2006. Since we're linking things from 2,000 years ago with contemporary culture throughout our Lenten journey, you may want to check out a documentary, *Dixie Chicks: Shut Up & Sing*. The feature-length film tells the story of the bluegrass-country band that, almost by accident, took an anti-war stance—then wound up with death threats and, for a while, a devastated career.

Here's how it all started: The super-popular trio of 30-something women was touring Great Britain in the run-up to the U.S. attack on Iraq. The women were so opposed to the war that they spoke out during a concert in London. Natalie Maines told the British audience, "Just so you know, we're on the good side with y'all. We do not want this war, this violence," and as the crowd roared, she added, "And we're ashamed that the President of the United States is from Texas."

The documentary opens with the Chicks—Martie Maguire, Emily Robison and Natalie Maines—reading emails that followed their Protest-Heard-'Round-the-World. One of them reads, "The Dixie Chicks suck! They ... should shut the *$@&$% up!"

Their career went from the Top of the Charts to the point at which, in at least one Southern town, bulldozers were crushing their CDs—and they were unable to tour for fear of death threats. For a time, the verdict was almost unanimously against them. In the documentary, they are shown withstanding a withering warning from a "consultant" from one of their corporate sponsors. Paraphrasing what that consultant tells the Chicks, envision a scene between Jesus and a marketing consultant for the Christian church, warning the rabbi: "At the end of the day, you are a great teacher, but you are also a brand—and you've got to stop telling these dangerous, depressing stories to people—or you know what will happen? Nobody's going to want to be part of a church with 'issues' circulating around it."

How is Jesus supposed to respond to that? "Well," he might say, "you could just leave the most controversial stuff out of the Lectionary."

And, even worse, in the documentary, the marketing consultant tells the Chicks to make nice in an upcoming television interview with Diane Sawyer. Natalie Maines describes the experience of those years this way: "The top of the world came crashing down."

We all know the rest of the story. The Chicks refused to "make nice" and they swept top Grammy Awards as a direct show of support for their gutsy exercise of free speech. These days, even Republican senators and officials in the U.S. armed forces agree that tragic mistakes were made in the rush to war in Iraq. As U.S. troops left Iraq at the end of 2011, a National Public Radio call-in show featured grassroots men and women nationwide sharing their disappointment with the way we invaded Iraq and conducted the long-running war. So if you watch the Dixie Chicks' documentary today, their courage may seem, in retrospect, less courageous. The tumult over the Chicks' incident in England may seem puzzling. It's worth seeing the film unfold, though, to see the anxious looks on the faces of these women—as their toddlers snuggle up with them and the women contemplate this cruel new world in which their stance for peace was literally drawing death threats to their families.

We can hear Jesus, in this parable, speaking to the men, women and children gathered around him that day. Yes, he's foreshadowing his death with the story, but more than that, he's probably gazing out at them with love in his eyes, saying: "Hey, listen up! Life is hard—and people can be incredibly cruel. So, please, be careful out there!"

When the Very Stones Become Spiritual IEDs

TODAY, WE RETURN TO contemplating stones—and we are about to encounter the most famous of the young rabbi's stone stories. We're already aware—from our earlier spontaneous glimpse of the stones during the Triumphal Entry into Jerusalem—that when Jesus directs our vision toward stones, he's actually pointing us toward the ultimate reality of God's Creation. If you're supplementing our journey with additional Bible reading, you'll find that the young rabbi is quoting Psalm 118 in the first part of this story—then, he's also echoing metaphors in Isaiah Chapter 8 and Daniel Chapter 2 about the power of solid stone to crumble the dangerous illusions that so often tempt us.

Let's check out Matthew's version of today's story. (John overlooks this story and Mark gives us only half of it.) In context, it's presented by Matthew and Luke as a further critique on the "Murder in the Vineyard" story. But it bears the marks of a group of teachings that probably were well known among Jesus' followers. It feels like a metaphorical way that Jesus liked to echo his larger view of the world—borrowing reflections on stones from ancient hymns and prophets. Matthew says:

Have you never read in the Scriptures: "The

stone the builders rejected has become the cornerstone; this is the Lord's doing and it is marvelous in our eyes"? Therefore I tell you: The Kingdom of God shall be taken from you and given to a people who will bring forth its fruits. And, anyone who falls on this stone shall be broken; but the person on whom the stone falls will be crushed into powder.

Most of us know the first part of that by heart, right? We've heard it preached—or even repeated in secular conversations—either as a general affirmation of our faith in underdogs, or as a specific foreshadowing of Jesus' ultimate triumph in the journey to Jerusalem. But—how often have we focused on the latter part of this teaching—that weird, Lewis Carroll-style double-speak: Watch out! Don't stumble over that stone! It may fall on you and crush you! It can't possibly do both, unless it's some sort of Improvised Explosive Device (IED) that can both impede our travel and blow up in our faces at the same time.

Dan Mulhern, who spent most of the last decade as Michigan's First Gentleman, also is an expert on leadership development. His book on the subject is called, *Everyday Leadership: Getting Results in Business, Politics and Life.* About halfway into the book, he offers some reflections that might be subtitled: Beware the Stone in your Pathway. He writes that one of the most devastating, substantial-as-stone IEDs in our lives are "the appetites that drive us" and he uses that phrase to describe all the non-rational compulsions we face in our lives, many of which can lead to great risk as we try to stumble around them secretly. Mulhern certainly is not alone in identifying a whole range of secretive addictions that can complicate, overwhelm and even destroy our lives.

When such secretive compulsions "go public," after the shock, isn't there always a moment of guilty realization when we admit that these are such common problems in life's roadway for most of us? Our compulsions and addictions vary widely, but they can become huge struggles. They're tough to overcome—and potentially explosive. Mulhern counsels would-be leaders to seek help. Shame is far easier to overcome than the devastation of— as Jesus puts it—letting the stone crush us when it falls. Or, as Mulhern describes these devastating stones: "How sad that we discover many of them through tragedy."

Flipping Coins with Our Future in the Balance

ARE YOU FEELING A little weary?

We're nearly one-third of our way into this Lenten journey today, but our weariness as Christians runs deeper than that, doesn't it? So often, as believers, we exhaust ourselves with the impression that, if we don't hold up the fragile pillars of our faith, the whole structure will come crashing down around us. At least one evangelical radio host has chosen a personal icon for his Web site of a knight in armor with a raised sword. Let's pray that it doesn't rain on all those steel joints, shall we?

"Spiritual warfare" is a popular phrase these days in many staunchly evangelical ministries. The world is so filled with evil, these preachers claim, that our only option is to stand alone or perhaps huddle up with a handful of like-minded Christians and wage spiritual war on our enemies. Unfortunately, this idea can become a self-defeating temptation, because it fails to recognize the vast diversity of the human community that God is compassionately summoning in each new generation. We're not supposed to stand alone, groaning under the weight of our armor, sweating as we clutch the sagging beams of our faith. Quite the opposite is true.

Psalm 90 tells us that God's kingdom is timeless and our lives are fleeting. While we're here, we're supposed to wisely reach out into the world and make compassionate connections. As the psalmist points out, however, this often is easier said than done.

The thing that Jesus encounters today is a perfect example of the struggle. In this case, the young rabbi rounds a corner and suddenly meets some very dangerous, very clever enemies who loom up like a flock of vultures. What they don't realize, when they try to fool him with a question about money and civic duty, is that one of this rabbi's most popular motifs is: Coins, Cash, Dole, Lucre, Moolah, Riches, Treasure, Wealth and Green. Here's how Matthew tells the story in Chapter 22:

> Then the Pharisees tried to entangle him. They sent their disciples to Jesus, saying: "Master, we know that you teach the way of God in truth; we know that you do not show preference to anyone. You are a fair man. Therefore, tell us: What do you think? Is it lawful to pay tribute to Caesar or not?"
>
> Jesus perceived their wickedness and said: "Why do you tempt me, you hypocrites? Show me some of this tribute money you would pay."
>
> They brought out a coin. And he said to them: "Whose image and inscription appears here?"
>
> They said to him: "Caesar's."
>
> Then, he said to them: "Render unto Caesar the things that are Caesar's; and unto God the things that are God's." When they heard this, they marveled and left him— and went their way.

John Dominic Crossan and Marcus Borg wrote about this famous exchange in *The Last Week: What the Gospels Really Teach About Jesus's Final Days in Jerusalem*. Jesus nailed the vultures the moment they produced their coin, Crossan and Borg tell us. Fully observant Jews, at the time, wouldn't have been caught dead carrying Roman coins with human images on them. Instead, they should have carried other currency that lacked graven images. The moment Jesus' opponents fished out an imperial coin, struck with the emperor's face, the crowd would have turned against them. Already embarrassed to admit they had such coins, the young rabbi skewered them further with his crafty verbal jousting. His enemies had hoped he would commit a seditious act by urging a tax rebellion against the Roman authorities—a potentially deadly violation of the law—or they hoped that he would back down and support the Roman authority, thus losing his street credibility. Instead, he managed to do neither.

Generally, this passage has been preached down through the centuries either as a defense of civil authorities ("Jesus himself called for obedience to the government!"), or it has been preached as defending separation of church and state. The most striking insight raised by Borg and Crossan is that, far from siding with either claim, Jesus' verbal joust actually opens up a question that's big enough to cruise through in a 757. The lingering question is: So, what exactly does belong to the emperor—and what belongs to God? Who are we—as men and women in the civic, commercial and spiritual realms in which we circulate each day?

Who is raising these questions now? Everyone, it seems! For instance, the *New York Times* reported that Wal-Mart divides Americans into market segments, based essentially on our coins: For example, some of us are grouped as "brand aspirationals," who can't quite afford the famous brand names we'd like to own, unless we find them on sale; some are "price-sensitive affluents," who have bigger incomes but are always seeking smaller prices; and some are "value-priced shoppers," who can't afford much—and know it.

Or, flip open any recent magazine and you'll spot this timeless struggle. Here's an example: An issue of *The New Yorker* included a full-page advertisement with a strikingly beautiful photograph of an attractive couple of baby boomers exploring an exotic vacation landscape. How could they afford this slice of heaven? Because they had figured out the secret of successfully defining their lives, this advertisement for an investment company explained. Under the photo, this concept of life was illustrated by a diagram of two large, overlapping circles. One circle was labeled "People Who Want to Expand Their Investment Options;" the other was "People Who Want to Expand Their Horizons." The ad argued that "*you*" should position yourself in the attractively greenish area of overlap.

Apparently, we're supposed to wrap ourselves around both sides of the coin?!

Well, 2,000 years ago, Jesus also flipped a coin—and raised a troubling question about the faces that flashed from each side. What will the coin look like—when it finally lands in our palm today?

The Divine "Dramedy" of Those Wedding Tales

NOW, WE ENCOUNTER TWO truths about Jesus that may seem strange in these final weeks of his life. First, we are reminded how much he loved weddings! Second, we are reminded that, as a storyteller, he was a master of what we now call "dramedy."

No one has published the definitive history of this cultural fusing of comedy *and* drama: dramedy. But, the term now pops up regularly in stories about TV series and sometimes movies, too. One dictionary claims the term debuted in the 1970s, others say it arose in the '80s and blossomed in the 1990s. According to one history of television, the first official dramedy was *Moonlighting,* a mid-1980s comedy-mystery starring Bruce Willis and Cybill Shepherd—because the series was nominated for awards in both comedy and drama categories. Whoever coined the term, the key distinctions seem to be that there is no laugh track in a dramedy— and the characters are more realistic. Very bad things can happen in the midst of these otherwise light-hearted stories. These tales are more like—well, more like real life.

The most popular storyline in dramedies? Love and marriage. In the movie world, think of: *When Harry Met Sally* (1989), *Sleepless in Seattle* (1993), *My Best Friend's Wedding* (1997) and *Runaway*

Bride (1999). While you're at it, you may recall this blend going way back—to 1950s TV dramatic showcases and '50s films like Spencer Tracy and Elizabeth Taylor in *Father of the Bride.*

Two thousand years before anyone thought to coin a term for it, Jesus was a master of the genre. In Luke 14, Jesus attends a big banquet and becomes quite the raconteur, spinning tales about wedding banquets. That's the famous passage in which Jesus tells his hilarious story about guests invited to a great banquet who come up with every lame excuse in the book to keep from coming to the party. That prompts the Supremely Loving Host to "bring in the poor, the crippled, the blind and the lame" to replace the stubborn invitees.

Jesus' Four Weddings and a ...

It's in perfect keeping with this rabbi's character that—even in the final days of his life—Jesus spins three stories about weddings, then shares a fourth story about the complexity of multiple weddings. But watch carefully what's happening in these later stories! We all know the much earlier Luke version by heart, but the version that comes late in Jesus' life in the Gospel of Matthew is thrown into stark relief by the rabbi's new urgency in conveying to his followers the harsh realities of this world.

What's different in this version of the story? Dramedy.

First, instead of including the funny lines about the potential guests' excuses in response to the Host's invitations—Jesus now says that the Host's servants are murdered by those they were trying to invite. Yes, *murdered*! And what does the Host do in this version of the story? Just snort in disgust and then radically reorient the invitation list? No! In this version, "The king was enraged. He sent his troops, *killed* those murderers, and *burned* their city." Yes, we're talking mass murder over a rejected wedding invitation. We're in Mario Puzo *Godfather* territory here, it seems. Only then, says Jesus in Matthew 22, does the invitation go out "into the streets to gather all they found, both good and bad."

Perhaps what we're reading here is an extremely poignant version of a much-beloved tale in the rabbi's repertoire of stories.

He's told tales like this for years to illustrate what life in God's Kingdom truly means—a community with all the joy and crazy convergence of a big family wedding. We're invited to the party, not because we've earned an invitation by our status in society, but because the ultimate Host loves the pure joy of a wedding banquet—and wants everybody to be there from the outcast uncle who's sure to get drunk to the crazy cousin with neon-orange hair.

We're going to contemplate the meaning of this timeless metaphor—a wedding—from several perspectives as our journey continues, because Jesus kept returning to this particular thing again and again. But, today, let's think about the spiritual poignancy and potency of wedding imagery. There's something about weddings that makes us grin!

The rabbi telling these tales still is a young man by our standards—barely in his 30s—but he's lived several lifetimes during his long road trip through the Holy Land. Now, he's facing the toughest part of the road—and, frankly, the old stories he's told a hundred times are taking on the fierce edges of the real world. It was one thing to laugh about the goofy wedding guests when Jesus and his followers were just starting out on this long adventure. Now, the weight of the Roman Empire and the cruelty of the world is about to come crashing down upon this once-merry band. Now, we're hearing high drama in the choices those wedding guests make.

To what can we compare these final wedding tales in Jesus' life? Perhaps there's a modern parallel in Jonathan Wilson's biography of painter Marc Chagall. In Wilson's view, among Chagall's greatest passions in life was his love for his wife, Bella. Born to a family of much higher social status than Chagall's, Bella's family at first was disgusted by her choice of a poor, eccentric artist. But, if there is such a thing as a divinely blessed match, this seems to have been an ideal example. Bella was a writer, nearly as talented with a pen as Chagall was with a brush.

The couple escaped the horrors of the Holocaust—even as the earth-shattering horror of the *Shoah* defined Chagall's vision as an artist. Then, in 1944, Bella caught a lethal virus—and was dying.

The masterpiece Chagall completed shortly before she died was, "A Ma Femme" (To My Wife), a vast, surreal celebration of—a wedding. There was Bella, a welcoming bride on a couch, floating in a beautiful world swirling with candles, animals, angels and the heavens above. The image was full of life and joy.

Then, Bella died. That's the dramedy of real life. What unfolded spanned the entire spectrum from love and joy, through all the comic imagery Chagall could muster, to the inevitability of Bella's death. And so it was 2,000 years ago: The thing the rabbi was trying to describe to his followers was the passion of a no-holds-barred, desperate search for love and joy in a world of madness. Chagall described that passionate search in paint.

And so we still search today.

More Weddings with an Ultimate Fashion Tip

NOW WE ENCOUNTER ONE of Jesus' most startling wedding stories: the tale of the boorishly inappropriate wedding guest whose fashion flaw cost him his life. This tale is an appropriate stop along our journey in this era of turbulent political encounters around the world. In the United States, political parties are so polarized that candidates or office holders who take so much as a single step beyond the fashionable boundaries of their political party can pay with their careers. We aren't interested in touching off a partisan brawl during Lent, so let's consider an example of today's principle that happened some years ago. Remember the strange sight in one of our past presidential campaigns when Merle Haggard released a tune he wrote in praise of—Hillary Clinton. Whatever your political stance, you'll probably agree that Merle's leap from his familiar status as a right-wing icon to a balladeer for the Clinton camp was an occasion for a little head scratching. Who *is* this guy, really?

That's what the king in Jesus' story asked 2,000 years ago. Here's how the rabbi put it in Matthew 22:

> When the king came in to see the guests, he saw
> a man who had no wedding garments. And he

said to him: "Friend, how did you come here
without wedding garments?"
The man was speechless.
Then, the king said to his servants: "Bind him
hand and foot. Take him away and cast him into
the outer darkness. There shall be weeping and
gnashing of teeth."
For many are called, but few are chosen.

Follow the story's application a little further: What if we envision God as our Host at such a party? Just imagine if the Host, today, gets a good glimpse at all the foolish and inappropriate disarray in our lives. Jesus is setting a pretty high bar in this lesson he's teaching us. What he's saying in this bitterly cast satire is that he's simply fed up with people who show up in the heart of the kingdom, acting like they're entitled to the celebration and deliberately flaunting the call for a top-to-bottom make-over in their spiritual lives. The rabbi is using clothing as a metaphor for through-and-through spiritual sincerity—a metaphor that's sprinkled across the New Testament.

A good example is Galatians 3:27 in which Paul writes:

For as many of you as have been baptized into
Christ have put on Christ. There is no longer Jew
or Greek, there is no longer slave or free, there is
no longer male or female; for all of you are one
in Christ Jesus.

At least that's how it's supposed to be in this new kingdom. Perhaps the rabbi's angry edge here reflects what he already knows is looming on his horizon—cynical insincerity as far as the eye can see.

Have you heard Merle's song or the story behind it? Here's what happened: On his own, this grizzled Old Man of Country Music whose fans now call him simply "Hag" composed a ditty to encourage Hillary Clinton's run for the White House. When they heard this, countless "Hag" fans were eager to bind him hand and foot and throw him into the outer darkness. The rants and raves were extreme! Consider this comment that was posted to a Web page about the country singer:

> Poor Merle. I knew the liquor would get the best of him sooner or later. We've come a long way from 'Okie From Muskogee.'

And this:

> Merle, prepare to be Dixie-Chicked!

But what was curious among these attack posts were other fans asking for a more thoughtful re-consideration of this battle-scarred troubadour's spiritual journey. One compassionate fan wrote:

> While I may not agree with Merle Haggard, I do admire his moxie. Now I'll have to find his tune, listen to it and see if it was as divisive as Garth Brooks' "We Shall Be Free."

And this:

> Hey, if anyone can write a song about Hillary Clinton, it's Merle Haggard; the man knows life and understands people. Yes, even he has said that "Okie" doesn't reflect where he stands now. Any artist, who is really an artist, is always changing, always thinking and re-thinking his or her work, and their place in the world. To my knowledge, Merle Haggard quit drinking, long ago—that's how he made it to 70. Don't short-change the man.

That's the remarkable part of the Haggard story as it relates to our tale of the boorishly inappropriate wedding guest. The man who Jesus described in this wedding story as only fit for the outer darkness had showed up at the party with a sense of entitlement and without the least attempt to truly clothe himself in the new kingdom's spirit. Haggard's fans were debating the exact nature of

Haggard himself, how he had clothed himself through the years and the true meaning of his song in 1969 that became an anthem of the exclusivist right wing in the Vietnam War era.

The thing Jesus was pointing out in this story of the boorish party guest turns out to be yet another timeless and true struggle, as potent today as it ever was.

After all these centuries, Jesus keeps asking: Who are *you*, really?

A Surprisingly Diverse Wedding Album

FINALLY, WE COME TO the end of this Wedding Trilogy with the most puzzling—and perhaps the most important—of Jesus' three tales about marriage at this point in our journey. As is often the case in the Gospels, his response is cast as a retort to his critics, but this passage in Matthew 22 and similar passages in Mark and Luke have the ring of oft-repeated responses from this rabbi when the complex issue of an afterlife is raised.

We can envision, years afterward, Jesus' followers saying to themselves: Hey, do you recall how Jesus always talked about the mysteries of Heaven? Remember how people always were pressing him, wanting to nail down the details, always trying to trip him up about how resurrection works? Remember that day when some critics came to Jesus, saying:

> Master, Moses said that if a man dies, having
> no children, his brother shall marry his wife
> and raise children for his brother. Now, there
> were seven brothers, and the first died, leav-
> ing his widow with no children. So, having no
> children, the widow married her husband's
> brother. Likewise, the second brother died, and

the third—right through to the seventh brother.
And, last of all, the woman died.
Therefore, in the resurrection, whose wife shall
she be of the seven? They all were married to her.
Jesus answered: "You are wrong. You do not
know the scriptures nor the power of God. For
in the resurrection, people neither marry, nor
are given in marriage, but they are as the angels
of God in Heaven. Considering the resurrection
of the dead, haven't you read what God said: 'I
am the God of Abraham, and the God of Isaac,
and the God of Jacob.' God is not the God of the
dead, but of the living."
And when the multitude heard this, they were
astonished.

In other words, Jesus dismissed such speculation as virtually irrelevant—as if such logic puzzles are beyond human comprehension, anyway. It would be far better, Jesus ultimately suggested, to think as God thinks about humanity—and pay more attention to the things in front of us in this life. That's the most important thing right now, Jesus said, because: God is not the God of the dead, but of the living.

The scriptures say the crowds "were astounded" at such teachings. Perhaps a better way of putting it: They were awestruck—in the sense of being intrigued and yet mystified by what the rabbi was saying.

As usual, Jesus is saying many things—but, in particular, Jesus is pointing out a profound and timeless spiritual truth. It's this: Ultimately, there are two kinds of people in the world—those who are not satisfied until they can logically grab hold of one single truth in their minds—and those who can hold more than one spiritual thing in their mind and heart at the same time. In 2011, the friction between those two kinds of people spilled over into a firestorm of criticism from evangelicals over Rob Bell's book, *Love Wins*. The book is a profoundly Christian reflection on the nature of heaven and hell—but it is framed in Rob's expansive view of God's universe as embracing many truths. For single-truth evangelicals, Rob was publishing heresy. Some online attacks on Rob amounted to verbal violence.

So, today, we are encountering Jesus himself telling people that we need to embrace multiple truths—or at least not lock ourselves away in fruitless logic puzzles pursuing a single truth. Trying to define the structures and the rules of heaven is a timeless temptation. Poets and prophets and ordinary parents have tried. In this story, Jesus is refusing to answer the question with a clear description. Instead, Jesus is saying that God's creative power is vast and mysterious enough that—yes, people can define their lives and their relationships one way on Earth; and in the next life ... well, Jesus says, in the next life people will be different in a mysterious new way—somehow like the angels. Contradictory? It may seem that way. We ask: How can a person wind up in heaven, identifiable as themselves, yet somehow completely different? How can we leave this puzzle unresolved?

And Jesus says: Just live with the puzzle. For now, there are enough things to concern us in the world close at hand.

The Rev. Dr. Charles Adams, the longtime pastor of Hartford Memorial Baptist Church in Detroit, visited the University of Michigan to lecture about the significance of African-American churches in U.S. urban history. As he talked about the distinctive history of the black church, Adams also wound up focusing on the need to unify communities—"for the good of aaaaaalllll the people," he repeatedly said, drawing out that word, "all," over and over again.

Why is that so hard? Adams asked rhetorically. The problem doesn't lie in the basic, tangible principles of religion, he said. Virtually all faiths teach us to love God and to love humanity—and virtually all faiths call for compassion to be shown to the poor, hospitality to strangers, peace to those in conflict and liberation to those who are oppressed. Those broad principles unite us, he argued. The problem comes, Adams said, when we try to define God too narrowly: "God becomes a problem if we claim to have the only valid description of God." There's not a more prominent Christian preacher in America than Adams and yet Adams refuses to use his stature and authority to narrowly define one way of understanding the faith. Instead, he echoes Jesus' call for an expansive vision.

Or perhaps it takes a secular voice to clear this debate from the debris of endless Christian in-fighting and express this truth more concisely. Former U.S. Secretary of State Madeleine Albright took a stab at this in her memoir, *The Might and the Almighty: Reflections on America, God and World Affairs.* She recalled appearing on a panel of experts with Holocaust scholar and author, Elie Wiesel, when he raised the question: Who is the unhappiest figure in the Bible? As Albright recalls it, Wiesel said that the unhappiest must be God—because of all the tragedies committed in God's name.

Powerful stuff, indeed! And a fascinating filter through which to glimpse fresh meanings from Jesus' words 2,000 years ago.

Jesus said: "Have you forgotten? Have you not read? God is God, not of the dead, but of the living." And God is God of many things—the whole cosmos, all Creation—a truth so vast that we cannot hope to hold it all within one human mind.

Finally, We Get the T-Shirt!

WHAT'S ABSOLUTELY DIVINE ABOUT our Lenten journey with Jesus is that he is not leading us exclusively on a pilgrimage through pain—despite what Mel Gibson showed us in that tough-to-watch movie a few years ago. This young teacher who is guiding our journey is a spiritual sage. He's ahead of his time, it seems—either that or perhaps ...

Perhaps he likes to teach about the things that are most important—in a timeless way. Think about the things that we've already heard Jesus talking about—stones, coins, trees, weddings. The substance of his message rests on timeless things. Even his style of teaching is timeless. Consider, for example, today's exchange with other wise Jewish leaders in Jerusalem. According to Matthew 22, some Pharisees struck up a conversation with Jesus and one of them asked:

> Teacher, which commandment in the law is the greatest?
> And Jesus said: "You shall love the Lord your God with all your heart, and with all your soul, and with all your mind. This is the first and great commandment. And the second is like it: You

shall love your neighbor as yourself. On these two commandments hang all the law and the prophets."

Many of Jesus' conversations, at this point in our story, have an aggressive edge to them. People are out to get this man who they regard as a troublemaker in their midst. Some would like to ensnare him in deadly traps. But this particular exchange wasn't disrespectful in itself. It was a common way of speaking with a rabbi—trying to draw out how this particular teacher understands the core of the faith.

It is well known that the great Rabbi Hillel—who lived and taught in the same part of the world, probably in the generation just before Jesus' time—welcomed such challenges from the people he encountered. It was common to describe this particular rhetorical challenge as: Explaining the Torah in the time it takes to stand on one foot!

Hillel's famous response to this challenge, which is repeated to this day, sounds remarkably like a portion of Jesus' own response. Hillel said: "What is hateful to you, do not do to your neighbor. This is the whole Law; the rest is merely commentary. Go! And, learn!"

Now, it is pointless to argue who originated such lines, because neither teacher originated them. These principles are the timeless core of our faith. The first commandment in Jesus' reply to the Pharisees is simply a direct quote from Deuteronomy 6, for instance.

Let's not mire ourselves in such details—and miss the creativity involved here. As we pause and smile over the wisdom of Jesus' Great Commandment to his followers, we also should celebrate the brilliance of these great sages in recognizing that brevity itself is a spiritual virtue! And talk about a timeless value—just look around at the headlines in our era. Look anywhere! You'll see signs of this news.

As Americans, we are so compulsive about accumulating and storing stuff that we are quite literally overflowing our homes! We're so obsessed with documenting our own lives that our

DVDs, hard drives, thumb drives and other digital data are too vast, in most cases, to ever go back and re-examine it all within the remaining time in our lives.

That's just our digital accumulation! We're even more frightening when it comes to saving real life stuff. A *New York Times* story by Suzanne Gannon, headlined "Hooked on Storage," detailed just how outrageous we've become with our self-absorbed consumption. For instance, Gannon reported, right now Americans have leased more than 2 billion square feet of storage space outside of our homes. That's more than twice the size of many American counties!

What are we saving?

I like the way *Wired* magazine editors put it in a special issue they published on Americans' "Snack Culture." They never mention Hillel or Jesus, but the editors do argue that Americans are desperately addicted to speed in their media messages, these days. Have you seen the TV commercials featuring guys staring at the latest flashes that come across their cell phones even as a major sporting event takes place around them? Various outsiders try to break into their phone-focused circle of friends, but the friends sneer at each newcomer: "You're sooo 30 seconds ago!" In fact, our lives are sooo oversaturated that—for better or worse—sound bytes may be the only way to get through to most of us. *Wired* summed the whole thing up this way: Now, "the T-shirt *is* the Message."

If you're having trouble hanging in there with us as we slowly make our way along these ancient roads around Jerusalem—at least we have the comfort of knowing that Jesus certainly would understand our restlessness. In fact, already in this Great Commandment today, Jesus essentially is swinging by the Jerusalem gift shop and giving us the T-shirt he wants us eventually to carry home from this long, wondrous trip!

Teacups, Tombs and a Timeless Howl from Bono

What should I make of a virtue that is in vogue yesterday, which will be discredited tomorrow—and becomes a crime across the river? What to make of truths that are bounded by mountains, but are false to the world beyond?
—16th-Century French essayist Michel de Montaigne

You blind fools! For which is greater—the gold in the Temple or the Temple that sanctifies the gold? ... You blind guides! You strain out a gnat and swallow a camel!
—1st-Century Rabbi Jesus of Nazareth speaking
to the crowds around Jerusalem

TODAY, WE COME TO a collection of the young rabbi's sayings about the deceptive appearance of things. It's easy to miss the significance of this next portion of our journey—and to misunderstand our guide's teachings—unless we understand that he's talking about the dire spiritual cost of deceptive appearances. He's talking about hypocrisy—and more.

Many Bibles introduce this section with headings like: "Jesus Denounces Scribes and Pharisees." This collection of sayings, as presented in the 23rd chapter of Matthew, is cast as a spat between Jewish groups—that is, between Jesus' band of Jewish followers and people from other Jewish groups. But read the whole chapter and think about it for a moment. Does this read like a single sustained attack delivered on a single afternoon? Perhaps it unfolded that way, but our guess is that Matthew has collected into this one stinging sermonette a whole series of the young rabbi's well-known sayings about hypocrisy.

Whatever its origin, this is a rhythmic, repetitive series of warnings and we need to consider the parts of this talk within Jesus' whole body of teaching. Overall, Jesus warns against those who "do not practice what they teach." Their hypocritical "front" is hard to maintain, he argues—like shouldering "heavy burdens, hard to bear."

Going down this pathway becomes a self-deceiving, self-defeating pilgrimage, he warns. Those who behave this way become "blind guides." And returning to his popular theme of coins and precious metals, Jesus says that it's very easy to confuse the glittering gold on the altars we build with the true faith symbolized in the altar itself. That's the context in which he delivers this blast:

> Woe to you ... hypocrites! For you clean the outside of the cup and the platter, but inside these dishes are hidden extortion and excess. ... First, clean out the insides, so that the outside of them will also be clean.
> Woe to you ... hypocrites! For you are like white-sided tombs, which indeed appear beautiful on the outside—but inside are full of dead men's bones and corruption. Even so, you outwardly appear righteous, but inside you are full of hypocrisy and iniquity.

So, here's the obvious part of this spiritual truth: The perfect set of china—all the perfect façades we display to the world may appear beautiful for a time, but there's an extremely high cost for maintaining such a display while concealing the oh-so-common failings in our lives.

And, there's more here. Overall, what Jesus is urging his followers to consider is this hard-to-swallow truth: The glue that holds our communities of faith together isn't found in our fancy public displays. What's most important in holding our lives together, he argues, is digging beneath the surface to share our complex interior lives with each other.

Two thousand years later, U2's Bono said the same thing in his famous "Preface to Psalms," written a decade ago for the landmark *Pocket Canons* project. For this famous edition of pocket-sized portions of the Bible, Bono described the Psalms as the world's oldest collections of "blues." He said that the Psalms are still so compelling to people, after thousands of years, because they represent a sacred place where it is appropriate to spend some time throwing our heads back and wailing to God about our pain.

Bono's "Preface to Psalms," now collected in a book called *Revelations*, says that the Psalms connect in such a visceral way with our lives after thousands of years because they voice our need to cry out to God about the agonizing conflicts we face. Bono writes that he still hears Psalms—he hears authentic cries to God—at the heart of some great musicians' works today. "I hear echoes of this holy row when unholy bluesman Robert Johnson howls 'There's a hellhound on my trail!' or Van Morrison sings 'Sometimes I feel like a motherless child.' Texas Alexander mimics the Psalms in 'Justice Blues': 'I cried Lord my father, Lord-eh Kingdom come. Send me back my woman, then thy will be done.'"

In other words, there is no pretense here, no hypocrisy—a model of prayer as the utmost in honesty. Not a false teacup left on the psalmist's shelf! Therein lies Jesus' ultimate teaching, doesn't it? Deceptively clean teacups may look impressive. But what truly defines us as individuals is the tension between the messy journey of life—and the ideals toward which we are stumbling. Bono is right. That universal tension in each human life, when honestly and eloquently expressed, is what connects with real people in popular music. It's what creates true community.

As our Lenten journey nears its center point, are we starting to see Jesus' themes resonating, echoing and circling back in our journey? Remember that early scene in Bethany, when Jesus' followers were horrified by a woman who threw protocol to the winds, literally let her hair down and poured perfume over his feet?

What did Jesus do? Rebuke her for the embarrassing sincerity of her disorderly display? No, of course not. Clearly, Jesus never stood on protocol. His eye never was on the gold, the tomb, the cup—but on the hearts within us.

For that, with Bono, we are thankful to this day.

Jesus Puts in a Good Word for Ssss-Snakes!

You serpents!
You generation of vipers!
How can you escape the damnation of Hell?

—Jesus of Nazareth

NEARLY HALFWAY THROUGH OUR 40-day adventure, we're deep in what we might call Act II of our drama—and the multi-layered nature of our rabbi is becoming apparent. Yesterday, we read about Jesus' lengthy harangue against hypocrisy—a straight-forward rant. But, Jesus also is striking notes in his words and actions that echo what unfolded earlier in his ministry—and what lies ahead of us, as well.

Today, in the 23rd chapter of Matthew, Jesus shocks us with— serpents! As amazing as this may seem, Jesus is the only major figure in the Bible to put in a good word for serpents! We all know that these reptiles have a dreadful reputation in the Bible from that horrific debut in Eden that ranks among the most famous scenes in global arts and letters. By later passages in the Hebrew Scriptures, the slithering bogeymen of Genesis grows like a child's worst nightmare into giants like in Leviathan: the crooked serpent, the dragon that dwells in the deep. To make matters worse for serpents, Jesus' Jewish heritage lay in communities of farmers and herders who regarded snakes as natural enemies.

The best that can be said of serpents in most biblical texts is that, someday, they may be rendered harmless, grazing for the rest of their lives on the dust, instead of flesh. (Check out Isaiah 65:25.) Even Jesus in Luke 10 repeats this kind of ancient promise that, someday, snakes will be harmless to the faithful. It's one of those quirky metaphors that, to this day, fuels the evangelical fervor in a handful of Appalachian churches where snake handling occurs as part of revival services.

But Jesus also said something unique in an earlier passage of Matthew (10:16, his famous "good word" about serpents): "Behold! I send you forth as sheep in the midst of wolves. Therefore, be wise as serpents and harmless as doves."

Of course, that's one of those lines that's now truly timeless. A couple of centuries ago in the time of the American Revolution and the founding of Methodism, that comment by Jesus underwent a major revival. It showed up in Revolutionary writings, but it also was a favorite of John Wesley in London. Knowing something about the Wesley brothers, it makes perfect sense that John would gravitate toward the image of Christians as combining purity of motives with a smart, discerning and even mysteriously clever style. Among other things, Wesley was a veteran street activist in the form of pamphleteering—which functioned something like the blogs of that era. It was in the form of a street pamphlet, for example, that Wesley finally came out staunchly against the practice of slavery.

Walk into the chapel that Wesley built in London in 1778 and you'll immediately gaze upward at the high pulpit from which Wesley preached. The pulpit was so high that it put him almost on an even footing with people sitting in the chapel's huge balcony. Then, your eye will move from the pulpit to the decorative reliefs along the balcony—a series of circular dove-and-serpent logos designed, it is said, by Wesley himself.

In this turbulent new century, evangelists including Tony Campolo and Rob Bell are reclaiming this kind of spiritually pragmatic approach that Wesley taught as a way for Christians to confront the thorny issues we face today. The meek and mild Jesus passively posed in thousands of paintings on the walls of Protestant churches is giving way to this much more complex image of Jesus. In books by Campolo, Bell and others, Jesus emerges as a smart, pragmatic teacher whose advice about serpents and doves makes perfect sense.

What does this dual role look like in a non-religious leader? Historian Randall Stross' fascinating book, *Wizard of Menlo Park*, deconstructs the towering myth of Thomas Alva Edison. To this day, Edison generally is lionized as the god-like inventor who brought the light of modernity out of our collective darkness. In his careful study of Edison's influence, Stross is not trying to slay the lion, but he is trying to explain why this gifted man attained legendary status. Stross explains that there was a complex network of scientists and strategic planning behind Edison's innovations. He cleverly managed his team's work and made himself the public face of their collective output. To put it very simply: He was both a dove and a serpent. As much as we may celebrate Edison as an ideal American innovator in technology and business, of course, his version of dove and serpent isn't religious leadership.

So, let's return to Wesley's life: Like Edison long after him, Wesley used strategic planning and a complex network of supporters to overhaul traditional notions about faith and spiritual expression within churches. When Wesley chose to tackle a deeply troubling issue, like the evils of slavery in England or cruelty to animals, he used full-force, serpent-like strategies to strike out in the public square with his religious opposition. As Francis Asbury (the pioneering American Methodist bishop in the late 1700s) began to unfold Wesley's Christian teachings and strategy on this side of the Atlantic—Methodism exploded across the new nation. Through the early 1800s, Methodism looked like it might remain the dominant national form of Christianity in the United States.

That it failed to maintain that creative spiritual momentum wasn't Wesley's or Asbury's fault.

So, just a reminder today that it's all too easy to shudder at the serpent along the road—and dismiss this slithering thing as an eternal threat. But, remember: The serpent wasn't always despised—not even by Jesus himself.

Envisioning a Mother's Wings—and Her Pain

THE SERPENT WASN'T THE only creature that our rabbi drew upon in his teaching. Jesus is also the only major figure in the Bible to use the mother hen—a chicken—in his teaching. In two of the Gospel accounts, he summons up the image of a hen as a metaphor for his compassionate love of humanity. In Jesus' heartbreaking lament over Jerusalem in Matthew 23 and Luke 13, the rabbi cries out in desperation:

> O Jerusalem! Jerusalem, you who killed the prophets and stoned those who were sent to your aid! How often have I wished to gather your children together, even as a hen gathers her chicks under her wings—yet you would not allow it!

As with serpents, Jesus seems to be alone in the entire sweep of biblical text in putting in a good word for chickens. Of course, unlike the serpent commentary, which we examined yesterday, the hen wasn't as readily picked up by male evangelists down through the centuries. It seems to be only in more modern times that Jesus' empathy for feminine perspectives on spirituality is regularly noted by Bible commentators. This is the same rabbi, after all, who in the 16th Chapter of John's Gospel compares the looming pain and eventual reassurance of God's grace as similar to a woman's labor pains. Beyond merely referencing labor pain, Jesus goes on to describe how a mother, after her child is born, no longer dwells on the pain she suffered because of her joy at this new life. Jesus stands in a very small circle of prophetic voices in invoking such images. In Genesis, for example, the pain of childbirth is referred to as a kind of eternal curse, but Jesus talks here about looking past the natural process of labor pains to the creative promise beyond it.

Of course, many Bible scholars, including Marcus Borg, now write about the close association in Hebrew and Aramaic between the words for "compassion" and for "womb." Borg points out that Jeremiah also plays on these notes in his evocations of God's love. God's compassion is like a mother's love for her child, as intimate as the promise of a life within her womb.

Protective hens and labor pains? This is strange narrative territory in Gospels written by men and dominated by the hard edges of stories scattered with stones, swords, coins, angry masters and brutal murders. As we encounter the hen—and Jesus talking about birth pangs—we are hearing about things that hark back to other uncomfortable territory. Remember the awkward scene at the table in Bethany with the woman at Jesus' feet? This was a rabbi whose spiritual scope spilled out beyond the comfortable boundaries of his male followers and the later male chroniclers of his ministry. One wonders whether he talked like this regularly and we are only picking up scattered echoes of these metaphors in the Gospel accounts.

Remember how much of this timeless story is shaped and framed by women? Remember the women in the Nativity narratives who we have skipped past in our Lenten journey? And, if you are familiar with the Gospels, you know that there are women in key roles still ahead of us in the final act of our drama.

A terrific companion book, which might be an intriguing choice during the balance of Lent, is Lindsey Crittenden's *The Water Will Hold You: A Skeptic Learns to Pray*. There's reporting in Crittenden's memoir that has the excruciating ring of real life with conflicting desires and realizations about life's deeper meaning that only come from an impressive commitment to writing the truth, wherever that journey takes the writer. A passage early in the book, describing her relationship with her mother as she was growing up, is written as an honest chronicle of the back-and-forth experiences between two women, one young and one old, that veers from compassion and high hopes to moments of jarring misunderstanding and conflicting motives.

Then, when Crittenden, as an adult, must attend to her mother's lingering death from cancer, she describes how her mother reaches out and pulls her head close. Doesn't that sound like a mother hen drawing her chicks protectively beneath her outstretched wings—a sensual memory of the chicks' earliest experience of this world?

Such things are easy to overlook in this rabbi's final discourses here in Act II of our Lenten drama. So many powerful scenes lie ahead of us that it is easy to focus on our eager anticipation of those famous scenes—and miss such small beauties that he carefully takes time in the midst of our journey to stop and to summon so vividly for us.

Life Among the Tumbling Milestones

As Jesus walked out and was departing from the Temple, his disciples came to look at the buildings of the Temple with him. And, Jesus said to them, "Do you see all of these stones? Truly I say to you: There will not be left here one stone upon another; they all shall be thrown down."

—Jesus to his followers in Matthew 24:1–2

AS WE ROUND THE center point of our Lenten journey, we find ourselves once again in the midst of stones and, this time, we're talking about enormous, historic stones. Some of those Jerusalem Temple stones were bigger than a train car, historians tell us, and weighed hundreds of tons. As brief as this little passage may be, it surely was freighted with ominous significance in the Gospels—which most historians agree were written in the final decades of the first century. Even the earliest Gospel, Mark, probably wasn't written until the year 70, which is when stones truly were tumbling in Jerusalem.

That's when the Roman Commander Titus ended his siege of Jerusalem with the city in ruins and a fire consuming portions of the greater Temple in the heart of the city. From Jerusalem, he marched on the towering Dead Sea fortress of Masada and, in 73, even that stronghold fell to Roman forces. From these victories, Titus returned to Rome where he succeeded his father Vespasian as emperor.

Think about the convergence of these events. There are historical parallels. In 1944 and 1945, little-known Italian director Roberto Rossellini bravely emerged with a band of filmmakers who took to the streets of Rome, shooting footage of the final days of the German regime. His powerful docu-drama about the liberation of Rome, *Open City*, jolted viewers around the world. In February 1946, *New York Times* film critic Bosley Crowther caught a showing of Rossellini's film and described it as electrically charged with emotion, anger, determination and a deeply stirring "exaltation" that these people understood something about surviving destruction—and the rebuilding that was needed in the aftermath. Imagine those words from a film review more than 60 years ago—applied to our Gospel passage today, written for a first-century religious community recovering from the devastation of the Roman campaign.

In the late 1940s, Rossellini was a man on fire. He also traveled to Germany and created one of the early *Trümmerfilme* (rubble films) shot in the ruins of the German empire. He called that drama, *Germany Year One*. Soon, a host of other filmmakers were following his example, although one might ask: What else could they have done? Their studios themselves were in ruins and there were no budgets to build sets or even to buy costumes. These artists focused, for a number of years, on coming to terms with the fallen stones littering their world—because there was nothing else they could do that made any sense to them.

It took many filmmakers years of reflection before they fully came to terms with the spiritual devastation that had swept around the world. It took 15 years after the war's end for Vittorio De Sica to release *Two Women* in 1960, which won an Oscar for Sophia Loren's heart-rending depiction of an Italian refugee, who flees Allied bombs with her daughter and is brutalized by soldiers hiding in a church.

That's the same year, 1960, that Japanese director Akira Kurosawa released *The Bad Sleep Well*, a Japanese *Trümmerfilme* based loosely on ideas from Shakespeare's Hamlet combined with the stark, black and white look of American film noir. Kurosawa and his creative team were way out on a limb in making this movie. His studio even forced him to form an independent production company, just in case he had trouble completing the project. There were real risks involved, because Kurosawa was deliberately challenging a second imperious force that had gripped Japan after World War II—a ruling class of criminals who dominated many of the country's emerging industries.

The drama concerns a noble young man called Nishi, played by the great Japanese leading man Toshiro Mifune, who devotes his life to bringing down the powerful mob bosses who have taken over Japanese industry. He actually joins one kingpin's family and marries his daughter in his quest to bring justice to his homeland. But, as the tension mounts in this quest, Nishi winds up retreating from the gangsters to a series of bombed-out shelters where he recalls spending the traumatic final days of World War II.

Teachers and discussion-group leaders might want to take a look at *The Bad Sleep Well*. It won't spoil the film to explain that Nishi doesn't live to see the end of his quest. He is executed in the final scenes—but, oddly enough, Kurosawa never shows us his body. It's as if Nishi has ascended to a better place. Instead, the final 10 minutes of the film show Nishi's closest follower, frantic in his grief, showing other friends the stone-strewn ruins of the bomb shelter where Nishi suffered and died. The friend holds up fragmentary evidence—a broken flashlight, shards of broken glass and finally a garment shed by Nishi during his execution.

"Look!" the friend cries, weeping as he scrambles through the rubble. "The signs of his last stand against them! See! See! Here is where Nishi fell! Here is where they beat him! Here is …"

Well, the point probably is clear by now, isn't it? As we've said time and again, our Lenten journey is timeless and true because these spiritual lessons echo through the millennia and across cultural barriers. Think about our four Gospel chroniclers for a moment. If there were *Trümmerfilme* after 1945, then these four sacred texts might be called "Trümmer-Gospels." All were written after Jerusalem was in ruins. In today's passage from Matthew, when the young rabbi says— "See all these stones? Not one will be left upon another. All will be thrown down"—his words resonate through so much of human experience in so many ages.

Rumors of Wars and the Poetry of Joseph Brodsky

You shall hear of wars and rumors of wars. See that you are not troubled by them, for all these things must come to pass, but this is not the end. For nation shall rise against nation, and kingdom against kingdom; and there shall be famines, and pestilence, and earthquakes

—Jesus, talking to his followers in Matthew 24 as they sit on the Mount of Olives, across the valley from the Temple in Jerusalem.

"WARS AND RUMORS OF wars." It's another of Jesus' most memorable observations about the true shape of the world around us—like the falling of stones or the natural cycle of trees. But, it's so easy to completely miss his wisdom here, especially with a phrase so ominous that it has been deployed from comic books to novels; from movies to music; from paintings to political speeches—usually to scare the dickens out of an audience.

Try the exact phrase above in Google—"Wars and rumors of wars" (in quotes)—and you'll find hundreds of thousands of Web sites echoing these famous words. As your companion on this journey, let me warn you about this little Google experiment with

Jesus' words: **Beware!** Some of the pages that use the phrase are almost pornographic in their dire warnings of conflict, famine, plague and earthquakes. Some evangelists, these days, are gleeful in their use of these terrifying images to try to predict the stages of an end-times drama and, along the way, drive hesitant pilgrims toward the seeming safety of faith

To this, I say quite honestly: Blindness! As sure as our Lenten journey is timeless and true, it's also certain that almost any fashionable sage who claims to have unlocked the secrets of history—is blind

Consider the case of Francis Fukuyama, the one-time neoconservative philosopher who was the darling of "neocons" shortly after his 1992 best-seller, *The End of History and the Last Man*, in which he argued that liberal democracy was the triumphant culmination of all historical cycles. Things certainly did look pretty good nine years before 9/11—and Fukuyama was celebrated with such heady praise that, even after 9/11, he threw his weight behind calls to attack Iraq, arguing that we should go to war even if there weren't any weapons of mass destruction. Novelist Tom Wolfe summed up the fall of Fukuyama as a once-revered "prophet" suddenly being made to "look like a fool" by terrorists who never got the message that history was supposed to end as neatly as Fukuyama had hoped.

The point here is this: Our rabbi on this journey isn't pulling any punches in the way he's showing us the world. Get out your Bible and read this whole section of Matthew, or similar passages in Mark or Luke. Collectively, they're called "The Little Apocalypse" by Bible scholars, an odd nickname for the passage—reflecting that there are other apocalyptic pieces in the Bible as well. If you're not eager to get to sleep tonight and want more scary visions, then check out Daniel and, of course, the Christian Bible's famous finale.

What Jesus really was doing in passages like this was preparing us all for even the most cataclysmic changes in our world. Whenever I read this "wars and rumors of wars" passage, I think of one of my own mentors as a writer—and the very unlikely way that I met this wise man.

In the mid 1970s, I was among a group of University of Michigan Creative Writing students who were disappointed to learn that our poetry seminar would not be led by one of the leading lights in our division of the university, called Residential College (RC). Instead, we were to be shoved off on a Russian immigrant, rumored to have quirky habits like chain-smoking foul-smelling cigarettes. It wasn't even clear whether he knew much English.

So, the first evening of that nighttime seminar, we all wandered skeptically into an RC lounge where our class was to meet, draping ourselves over the beat-up easy chairs and frowning at the sour smoke already filling the room.

Poet Joseph Brodsky smirked at us, shook his head disdainfully, stubbed out his cigarette in an already overflowing coffee cup, lit another, inhaled, exhaled—and then asked in a thick accent: "So, who among you knows a Psalm?"

The silence was so complete we could hear his breath sucking through the cigarette. "I can wait," he said. And he did.

Then, a cigarette later, he repeated his plea. "Let's hear a Psalm. Surely you know them. You must. Because if none of you knows a Psalm—a single Psalm—then we have got so much more to memorize in this class than I had planned." He sighed wearily. The ominous word "memorize" transfixed us.

Finally, a brave young skeptic brushed the shaggy curls from his eyes and said, "This is a poetry seminar. Why would you expect us to memorize the Bible?"

Brodsky smoked his way through the rest of that cigarette. Then, he stubbed it out. Lit another.

At length, he said, "Because, someday, if you are sent to a prison camp—the poetry you carry in your memory may be your entire world. So, we must choose well what world we will carry, no?"

Of course, as students, we soon learned that Brodsky was emerging as a literary hero on a global scale. He had served 18 months of a severe Soviet prison term in a camp in remote northern Russia because he was self-educated and refused to limit his work to themes acceptable to the Soviet writers' union. The young Brodsky had refused to play by Soviet rules as an official writer, so he was charged as a "parasite." This "Kafkaesque" legal charge arose, despite the fact that he tried to work as a writer and translator. He wrote outside the official system. By definition, in the Cold War Soviet view of society, his refusal to bow to official pronouncements made him a criminal. Here is one exchange between the courageous young poet and the judge—a ruthless and clueless figure one might imagine from some John Le Carré novel.

> **judge:** And what is your profession?
> **Brodsky:** Poet. Poet and translator.
> **judge:** And who told you, you were a poet? Who assigned you that rank?
> **Brodsky:** No one. (nonconfrontational) Who assigned me to the human race?
> **judge:** And did you study for this?
> **Brodsky:** For what?
> **judge:** To become a poet? Did you try to attend a school where they train poets—where they teach—
> **Brodsky:** I don't think it comes from education.
> **judge:** From what then?
> **Brodsky:** I think it's(at a loss)—from God.

Think about this brave and inspired exchange. Does the exchange sound anything like another famous Jewish sage who lived, say, 2,000 years before Brodsky—who was equally innocent as a dove and wise as a serpent with those who interrogated and later conspired to condemn him?

For decades after this traumatic experience in the Soviet Union, Brodsky would tell his students, essentially this: Someday, there may be wars and, worse yet, rumors of wars. Like millions of others in lands around the world, you may be sent to a prison camp one day. So, the poetry in your memory may be your entire world. As the class unfolded in the RC that year, all of us in Brodsky's class memorized hours of poetry—especially Psalms and the works of Robert Frost.

Brodsky liked to describe Frost as, "The only American poet to truly understand the depths of the human spirit." Anyone who ever heard Brodsky recite *Stopping by Woods on a Snowy Evening* never forgot the inflection that wrenched the lines free from the dust of nostalgic Americana and made them, forever, an essential part of our world. Brodsky focused, like our rabbi on this Lenten journey, on clearly delineating the things we must remember.

Stubbing out a cigarette—and not lighting another—Brodsky would declaim:

Whose woods these are I think I know.
His house is in the village though;
He will not see me stopping here
To watch his woods fill up with snow.
My little horse must think it queer
To stop without a farmhouse near
Between the woods and frozen lake

And then Brodsky's voice would slow. A breath. A pause. And his voice would continue:

The darkest evening of the year.

Of course, most Americans know where this poem is headed—just as we know where Jesus' own teachings keep pointing us: toward moving on with our lives, whatever darkness we may be experiencing for a time, and continuing to compassionately build communities.

Even Robert Frost knew that this is the spiritual point of life, as he penned his final lines:

I have promises to keep,
And miles to go before I sleep,
And miles to go before I sleep.

Finding Joy in "The Physical World ... Dancing"

Then Jesus told them a parable: Behold the fig tree, and all the trees. When they send out shoots, you know that summer is nearly at hand. Truly, I say to you: This generation shall not pass away until everything is fulfilled. Heaven and Earth shall pass away; but my words shall not pass away.

—Jesus talks with his followers in Luke 21:29–33

REMEMBER OUR EARLIER ENCOUNTER with a fig tree a couple of weeks ago? If not, turn back to Chapter 9, where we tried to focus on a single tree amidst an abstract forest of interpretation.

Today, we find ourselves shouting, again: **Behold!** There's yet another fig tree on our journey. And this encounter was so memorable to Jesus' followers that it appears almost word-for-word in all three synoptic Gospels. It's true that John cuts out this particular scene from his version of the drama, but—right about this point in John's narrative—we get another famous floral metaphor: "I am the vine, you are the branches," Jesus tells us in John

15, and continues with his extended metaphor about the need to tend, prune, remain connected—and ultimately bear fruit in the vineyard.

Clearly, this rabbi was so deeply rooted in the things of this world that he wanted his followers to understand that they, too, could find larger truths by examining the wonderful parts of God's creation. Such discoveries, Jesus is teaching us, can spark a sense of awe and, then, a transcendent joy that can spill over into compassionate love.

Fancy terms for this, like "eco-theology," are buzzwords among progressive theologians and social activists. But what the young rabbi is showing us here is far more than a trend. It's a timeless struggle to keep our senses connected with truths far beyond our individual lives. It's almost as if—after warning us against the dangers of losing ourselves in "rumors of war" yesterday—Jesus goes further as he grabs a fistful of fresh fig shoots (or grape vines) and shakes them at us. Can you hear him almost shouting at us in the urgency of this message?

"See this? Look!" he is saying. "Here's the key to opening a spiritual doorway in the midst of your depression about the state of the world. Stop! Actually *look* at the world! And, in addition to all the horrors you'll see, you'll also discover that branches continue to sprout each spring! The cycles of creation continue! God never abandons us!"

Sound like a simple lesson? Well, just *look* at the world—and you'll find that people are struggling every day with this very issue. For instance, Big Sur, the near-legendary California landscape that has drawn artists, writers and other metaphysical seekers for generations, now is pricing such seekers out of the landscape. Once a haven for cabins and cottages, Big Sur now attracts builders of multimillion dollar homes with little room for the modest budgets of ordinary men, women and families.

America's most awe-inspiring landscapes have been evolving into playgrounds for the rich over many years, so we now need to protect natural outlets for the rest of us. On this very point, a beautiful art book by the Getty Museum in Los Angeles, *Guide to*

Imagery: Gardens in Art, is very much like a paperback version of Jesus' fistful-of-fig-tree lesson. It's refreshing and reassuring to remember, while flipping through the gorgeous pages of this book, that this spiritual concept isn't limited to a handful of sages. It's a timeless creative challenge. Remember Frederick Law Olmsted, the designer of New York's Central Park 150 years ago? The book shows early images of his masterpiece and explains that Olmstead believed that the health of our nation depended to a large extent on the design of our parks.

Hear a little echo there of themes in our rabbi's lessons?

Bill Henderson, the novelist and founder of the Pushcart Press, has heard those echoes resounding through the centuries in the hymns that are an inescapable part of Western Christian culture. In a sometimes-argumentative and sometimes-lilting memoir, *Simple Gifts: Great Hymns: One Man's Search for Grace*, Henderson writes about his life, his spiritual struggle with cancer—and his quest to come to terms with hymns he dislikes and those that he loves.

Henderson loves the natural world, so he feels especially drawn to hymns that capture the renewal of hope that can accompany a good hike in the woods. He may be a self-taught theologian, but he's also a discerning one. In fact, he argues that clergy have gotten several things wrong in their handling of hymns, including their seasonal limitations. In one of his most passionate pleas, he says that clergy should unleash Isaac Watts' "Joy to the World" from its Christmas ghetto so that it can be sung all year 'round. Perhaps we should pull it out and sing it as Easter approaches. In the hymn, Henderson says, Watts is conveying a powerful truth that "Fields, floods, rocks, hills, and plains repeat the sounding joy." Henderson calls this a powerful image of "the physical world … dancing."

Hear the echoes?

If not, think again about that passage in John in which Jesus compares himself to a vine. Remember how that ends? The young rabbi explains that, ultimately, he's waving this fresh foliage in our faces to make this point: "If you keep my commandments, you shall abide in my love; even as I have kept my Father's commandments and abide in his love. I have told you these things so that my joy might remain in you, and that your joy might be full."

Hear the echoes now?

Minding Our Lamps and a Visit from Archbishop Tutu

> The kingdom of heaven is like 10 young women, who took their lamps and went forth to meet a bridegroom. Five of them were wise; five of them were foolish.

That's how Jesus begins today's startling new story in this cycle of lessons about the kingdom he envisions. Just listen to his language here. He wants us to sit back and really think about this tale. It's classic storytelling, even in the cadence of its opening: Five of them were wise; five were foolish. It sounds almost as though we're in the midst of *Jack and the Beanstalk,* or perhaps *Little Red Riding Hood.* It's a story of suspense in which a potentially devastating event is looming that will affect the lives of both the foolish and the wise.

> Jesus continues: Those who were foolish took their lamps, but took no oil with them. The wise took oil in their vessels along with their lamps. While the bridegroom was delayed, they all

slumbered and slept. At midnight, a cry went up: "Behold, the bridegroom comes! Go out to meet him!" Then all those young women arose and tended their lamps. And the foolish said to the wise: "Give us some of your oil; for our lamps have gone out."

Here's where this story takes a very odd turn, if we assume that Jesus is talking about himself as the bridegroom in the center of this kingdom that he sees emerging. Listen carefully to what happens next:

But the wise replied: "No! There is not enough for us and for you; so go to someone who sells oil and buy some for yourselves." And, while they went to buy oil, the bridegroom came; those who were ready with their lamps went in with him to the marriage and the door was shut. Afterward, the other virgins returned, saying: "Lord, Lord, open to us!"
But he answered: "Truly, I say to you: I do not know you."
Therefore, keep watch, for you do not know the day or the hour when the son of man will come.

At this point, after the Alfred Hitchcock ending to our little tale, aren't we scratching our heads and murmuring: "Whaaat?!?" In this new story, the young rabbi is taking wedding etiquette a giant step further than the story in Matthew 22 about the boorishly inappropriate party guest. If you missed that one, jump back to Chapter 15 in our journey to read about the fate of that poor jerk. At least in that story, we could nod our heads knowingly at the end and say to ourselves: Well, it was his own fault! The guy was acting like he was entitled to the celebration, but he was deliberately flaunting the call for a top-to-bottom transformation in his spiritual life. Served him right!

But in this new story we've got a bunch of innocent young women cast into the outer darkness as the banquet hall's heavy wooden doors boom shut. Some translations refer to these young women simply as bridesmaids or virgins. Whatever they're called, it's hard to identify a flaw in this group of hopeful young women. They all showed up properly equipped. The worst that can be said about the foolish five is that they weren't as obsessive compulsive as the wise five about lugging along a spare tank of oil.

What's wrong here? Why doesn't Jesus' wedding party decide to pool the oil—or do without oil entirely? Where's that host who Jesus described earlier who's so generous that he throws open the doors of the banquet hall even to social outcasts? It's a troubling tale, no question, and only Matthew shares it with us. One wonders whether it wasn't just a little too challenging for the other Gospel writers, who left this one on the cutting-room floor.

The best reading of the tale we can envision, prompted by looking over an array of commentators who have pondered this scene down through the centuries, is that this is a story about the discipline of spiritual mindfulness. Barbara Brown Taylor likes to call lit "reverence." Consider: In this cycle of stories in Matthew, the rabbi has taken us from a stern warning over the spiritual fog that can come in an atmosphere of fear and "rumors of war"—to a plea for the need to clear our vision by taking a fresh look at the natural world around us ("See this fig tree sprouting"). And, now, he's driving home the conclusion—a lesson about the life-and-death nature of spiritual mindfulness.

If we don't prepare ourselves in each waking moment, the rabbi seems to be saying, we'll completely miss the banquet—and there's no easy way to make up for that lack of preparation by, at the last minute, desperately trying to siphon off a little spiritual oil from the next person's jug.

This must have been a puzzling lesson for Jesus' followers. These were men and women with a pragmatic view of human life. In their world, people were people—not esoteric, multi-layered creatures with separate realms of mind, body and spirit. Here was Jesus talking to them about a transcendent potential in their daily spiritual disciplines—a hard concept to grasp. But, he isn't alone in delivering this kind of teaching. Actually, some of the wisest prophets through the centuries have stressed this same principle.

The Buddhist monk and author Geri Larkin talks about this frequently. "Mindfulness is the surest path to happiness," she says, meaning that it's essential to live our lives fully alert to the world around us—so that our spiritual awareness is developing day by day.

One of the greatest practitioners of spiritual mindfulness in our present age is South African Archbishop Desmond Tutu, a sage who I've interviewed several times since the 1980s. My most memorable encounter with Tutu, however, was an entirely unexpected one that came during the worldwide Anglican Communion's gathering at Canterbury Cathedral a couple of decades ago, when reporters from around the world came to cover the bishops' historic debate on women's ordination. That particular conference opened with all the pageantry the British could muster—with long lines of Anglican bishops from all around the world marching into the vast nave of the cathedral in their vestments. The bishops from the UK in particular looked like a cast of characters from a Dickens novel, many with florid cheeks, severely cropped hair and a lofty tilt to their chins.

The opening session featured several talks in which bishops threw down verbal gauntlets on either side of the debate. And, when the bishops were ready to file out of the cathedral, the press corps hit the church doors first—hoping to rush back to the press center and write the latest news stories. However, as those of us in the press corps rushed for the doors—trying to outdistance the bishops who also were rising from their seats and forming up in their long rows to march away through those same doors—we wound up nearly colliding at the exit. And, as the very last member of the press corps, pushing open the heavy cathedral door—I recall the embarrassing moment: I was stuck there! I was the last reporter holding the door as the first of hundreds of bishops reached the exit. They rumbled and rustled past, chins high, eyes still aloof from the non-episcopal classes—no one even attempting to reach out and shoulder the door's weight.

And then ... then a firm hand came down on my shoulder; the weight of the big cathedral door was pushed free—and another shoulder was set to patiently brace the doorway. Looking into my eyes was Tutu. His chin was down. His eyes alert. Unlike most of his colleagues, he clearly was mindful of every soul in the crowd, even a journalist caught in such an awkward situation.

"You did not travel all this way to serve as our doorman," Tutu said warmly. "I will hold the door for the rest of them. And you? You have important work to do, now. Go. Write your story. I will stand here."

Now, that is spiritual mindfulness, even in the midst of a historic, international gathering with such major issues to contemplate. Tutu had trained himself not to miss even the smallest detail in lives on the periphery of his episcopal world. It is that same mindfulness—expressed in such a tiny way that day in Canterbury—that has shaped Tutu's entire approach to life. His daily discipline gave him the capacity to expand that compassionate vision to an amazing degree a few years later in 1995, when he was asked to chair the South African Truth and Reconciliation Commission. Now celebrated as a model for dealing with crimes against humanity in a just and compassionate way, Tutu's three years with the commission sorted out claims from more than 7,000 people. These were confusing claims that came from both sides in South Africa's long struggle toward freedom.

Perhaps Tutu's light was a divine gift in those years—but the truth seems to be that Tutu had carefully tended his lamp day after day, year after year, until it held the power to glow brightly under any circumstances.

So, how are our lamps doing at this point in our journey? Are they glowing? Have we packed enough extra fuel for such a long pilgrimage? Perhaps it is time to check our oil—and make sure we're preparing ourselves for the climactic scenes looming just ahead of us down the Lenten road.

In This Kingdom, Even Coins Change Value

WE ARE NEARING THE climax of what we might think of as Act II in our Lenten drama—and Jesus already is setting a new table for us. In this week of our reflections, he is turning from his long series of warnings about the spiritual discipline necessary in our individual lives—to a series of lessons in which he points out things that will help us grasp the larger dynamics of this new kingdom he envisions.

First, Jesus returns to one of his favorite metaphors: Coins, Cash, Dole, Lucre, Moolah, Riches, Treasure, Wealth and Green.

If you've skipped our earlier Lenten reflections on coins, you might want to look back at Chapter 7 and Chapter 13—because Jesus is far from finished with our consideration of these particular things. I especially like Mark's version of the first of three coin stories we'll consider this week, because of the wonderful way that Mark sets up the narration. We can picture the young rabbi, in Mark's story, perching himself somewhere in Jerusalem near the Temple—doing precisely what we're doing in this series—carefully observing what's happening in the everyday lives of people around us.

Here's how Mark tells the story in Chapter 12:

Jesus sat near the treasury and watched how people cast money into the treasury. Many who were
rich cast in much money. Then, there came a
certain poor widow, and she threw in two mites,
which make a penny.
And Jesus called his disciples to him, telling
them: Truly, I say to you, this poor widow has
cast more in, than everyone else who has cast
money into the treasury. For they all cast in out
of their abundance; but she cast in all that she
had—even all her living.

Now, any of us who've spent much time around a parish have
heard this story told and retold until we've distilled it to short-
hand. All we have to hear is, "the widow's mite," and we know the
tale, don't we? It's a classic story of Jesus' affection for the underdog—end of story.

But have we considered the subversive nature of this story?
Have we stopped to think about the strange twist in this tale,
coming from a rabbi who specializes in economic theory? Jesus
preaches frequently about Coins, Cash, Dole, Lucre, Moolah,
Riches, Treasure, Wealth and Green. He's even famous for posing
a theological conundrum, while flipping a coin in the palm of his
hand, that people continue to debate after 2,000 years. He posed it
this way: Caesar's face may be on the coins we hold, but how will
each of us determine what actually belongs to Caesar and what
belongs to God?

Perhaps you're uncomfortable hearing so much about money
in this Lenten journey? We all know the feeling. It's almost impossible to escape financial anxiety these days. The front pages of
our newspapers are turning into a litany of downsizing and lay-
offs. Most troubling of all, our entire economic framework has
been shifting for several years. In the past, we always trusted that
our homes would increase in value—now they've decreased in
value and millions have oversized mortgages hanging like mill-
stones around their necks. In the past, we assumed that gasoline

always would flow freely around the world—now historic shifts are underway across the oil-producing world, raising questions about whether oil will continue to flow from many trusted ports.

Here's the good news! Two thousand years ago, Jesus taught his followers that core values *will shift* in God's kingdom. Things we thought were of substantial value will fade before our eyes and things we thought were virtually useless—like the poor woman's sacrifice at the treasury—will become supremely valuable.

What a strange new kingdom lies before us!

In recent years, an international conference drew thousands of pastors to the Rev. Rob Bell's Mars Hill Bible Church in Grandville, Michigan. During those three days, Bell spent a lot of time talking about the "New Humanity" Jesus is calling into being—across all ages. Rob told the crowd that our motives should not be that we— who are among the wealthy—finally are agreeing to be good sports in listening to the grim news about poverty or that we are not reluctantly agreeing to shoulder our spiritual burdens. No! Rob told the crowd that we need to do this because our very salvation depends on figuring out the shifting values in this new kingdom.

Or, as Rob put it that day: "When you finally know somebody who is poor, roughly 2,000 verses of the Bible start to make sense."

Who Do You Trust: Uriah or Yunus?

DO YOU KNOW THESE names: Uriah and Yunus? The former ranks among the oiliest villains in all of literature—although for most of his infamous life in *David Copperfield*, Uriah Heep appears to be the ideal clerk in a law firm. The latter ranks as a saint in global economic justice—although Muhammad Yunus' fame has surfaced all manner of critics who are taking shots at his integrity. The two may seem to be polar opposites—one fictional and one real; one British Christian and one Bangladeshi Muslim; one centuries old and one contemporary. In truth, both are models of shifting fame and fortune.

And, shifting fortune is one of Jesus' central themes throughout the Gospels. As values shift in this new kingdom Jesus envisions, he already has warned us not to evaluate people based on their monetary wealth. Then, in his story today, he warns that we shouldn't assume that we have a right to hang on to the resources we are given. They're not ours, Jesus is saying. Whatever things we receive in this life are merely entrusted to us for the good of the entire community.

You know this story by heart, don't you? It's the "Parable of the Talents," although we're willing to bet that none of us knows exactly what a "talent" is worth without checking reference works. Even then, it's confusing to figure out an exact modern equivalent. In the Roman Empire, a talent was a measure of weight and the term "talent" referred to a mighty big pile of silver or gold. One source says it's about 75 pounds of precious metal; another source says 100 pounds. Scholars disagree about precise values—except that a talent was a whale of a lot of dough!

Jesus' story about a master who gives his slaves a number of talents to manage for him is likely to have prompted some raised eyebrows in the crowd. Clearly, this was a tale of epic proportions. This master was tossing around big money! What would these lucky slaves do with all the loot he was handing over to them? In Matthew 25, Jesus says:

> The kingdom of Heaven is like a man traveling
> into a far country, who called in his servants and
> gave them his goods to keep. To one, he gave
> five talents, to another two, and to another one;
> to every servant according to his ability. Then,
> straightway, he took his journey.

OK, we're following Jesus so far. After that story yesterday, it's clear why the story opens with each slave getting a different amount. Values are shifting, Jesus says. Justice doesn't involve equally dividing every pie—some seeming inequalities will occur even in this new community. Don't keep your eyes on the exact dollar amounts, the rabbi is saying. Instead, watch the overall flow of money. Why? Well, Jesus continues:

> Then the servant who had received the five tal-
> ents went and traded with these talents and
> made five more five talents. Likewise, the servant
> who had received two also gained another two.
> But the servant who received one went and dug
> into the Earth—and hid his lord's money.
> Then, after a long time, the lord of those servants
> came and reckoned with them. The servant who

had received five talents came and brought out his other five talents, saying: "Lord, you delivered five talents to me. Behold, I have gained five more."

His lord said to him: "Well done, you good and faithful servant; you have been faithful over a few things, I will make you ruler over many things. Enter into the joy of your lord."

The servant who had received two talents came … and the same thing happened with the lord.

But, what about the "third guy"? Well, we know already, don't we? If you're familiar with Charles Dickens' *David Copperfield*, then you recognize this third guy was the "Uriah Heep" of the bunch. Probably, he was figuring his master might never come home, maybe the accountants keeping track of those talents might forget about him. And, since he'd hidden his treasure—the scheming little wretch might wind up keeping this pile of precious metal for himself. Of course, this Uriah Heep in the talents story is too unctuous to admit his own avarice. His pompous oration goes like this:

Lord, I knew that you are a hard man, reaping where you hast not sown and gathering where have not planted. I was afraid—and hid your talent in the Earth. And, behold! Now, you can have what is yours back again.

But his lord answered: You wicked and slothful servant. If you know me, you should have put my money out into the exchanges, then when I came home I would have received mine own with interest. So, take the talent from this man— and give it to the servant who has 10 talents now. For everyone who has shall be given more and will have an abundance, but he who has nothing will find what he has taken away.

Then, the lord said: Cast this unprofitable servant

into outer darkness. There shall be weeping and gnashing of teeth.

Wow! There are a whole bunch of people getting their "just desserts" in Jesus' recent stories. How many people have been tossed out into that outer darkness so far? This is like the big showdown in a 1950s western, right? Frankly, what Jesus is saying is hair raising, isn't it? He's saying that the slave who doesn't realize that resources should keep circulating through the community has, in effect, invalidated his own life! Remember, in most accounts this servant is actually a slave—by definition a valuable human being—whose life the Master is tossing out the back door.

It was his own fault, Jesus is saying. By pulling out of the community and entrenching himself in his own little world of greed and self-fulfillment, he's not even worthy of life. Now, that's an in-your-face indictment of a whole lot of us, isn't it? When Jesus told this tale, it must have jolted his audience, because—let's be honest—most of us are tempted toward Uriah Heep's self-interest, aren't we? Haven't we ever caught ourselves curled up in our cubicles, feeling sorry for ourselves over how the world's been unfair and we're due every single penny that comes our way? Even as we admire compassionate Christian activists, we also chuckle over the truth that American culture encourages us to pursue our own egoism. We may sometimes despise our own petty competitiveness in the public square, but come on—we know it's true. There's a little Uriah in most of us. That's why *The Office* was such a hit and Dilbert comics are so funny!

One of the greatest contemporary illustrations of Jesus' message is actually a Muslim: the Bangladeshi economist and 2006 Nobel Peace Prize winner Muhammad Yunus. Born in 1940, Yunus earned his doctorate from Vanderbilt University in the U.S. and returned to his homeland during the mid-1970s famine, his mind bursting with creative ideas and his heart aching at the devastation in his country. Much like the young rabbi whose teachings we're considering in our Lenten journey, Yunus had to walk a creative tightrope to reach his historic innovation: the creation of a global system of micro-finance. On the one hand,

Yunus had to avoid Muslim critics of usury, the religiously unacceptable business of lending for financial gain. On the other hand, he had to convince business executives that their future depended on helping the impoverished masses climb out of the forgotten depths—and into the main streets of the larger community, once again.

As Jesus talks about this challenge, it's clear that he sees the sharing of money as a natural extension of his expansive custom of creating community by eating and drinking with friends and strangers. Everything must be shared, he is teaching: food, drink—and money, too!

As Yunus talks about the birth of his idea, which now is celebrated around the world for its compassionate genius, he admits that it's this nitty-gritty notion of sharing with disreputable strangers that was his biggest roadblock. In interviews, Yunus likes to describe the first time he met with a banker and proposed that the executive help him to set up a system of small loans to help Bangladesh's poorest families.

As Yunus recalls the exchange, "When I proposed to him that he lend money to the poor people in a village—it was like he was falling from the sky! He was shocked! He didn't believe I had even said that! He said, 'No! It can't be done! It can't be done!'"

Why? Yunus says the banker told him, "Because, poor people are not credit worthy."

That's when it began to dawn on Yunus that this entrenched problem was deeper than a question of good business practices. There was a spiritual dimension to this problem. Yunus' greatest genius was his declaration that poor people needed no collateral to receive a loan. The value lay in themselves, he declared: "The fact that you are a human being is a good enough introduction for us," he said.

Yunus was correct. When poor people are invited into a microfinance system, designed like a compassionate social network, they have a better than 99 percent return on loans! Now, many charitable agencies and even some governments around the world are eager to funnel funds into his vision of a better community.

It's that affirmation of trust—the same affirmation Jesus made 2,000 years ago—that was so powerful in spreading Yunus's message around the globe. It's such a radical notion that, in recent years, various critics have popped up trying to topple Yunus from his pedestal as a prophet. At least one major documentary film, produced in Europe, accused Yunus of corruption and caused a worldwide stir—until the film's "investigation" turned out to be based on entirely bogus information. Yunus has been dragged into court repeatedly by people who claim he has not met their needs in one way or another.

Sounds a bit like what Jesus received for all his trouble as a compassionate prophet, doesn't it? Yunus' life story is far from over, but we know the rest of the tale of Uriah Heep: Like Jesus' servant 2,000 years ago, Heep wound up justly punished.

The message is as radical—and as true—as when Jesus proclaimed it two millennia ago: For to all those who have a proper heart for the community and a proper mind for our precious resources—more will be given. Our faith is that, eventually, there will be an abundance shared by all.

Values and Villains—Judas and Leni Riefenstahl

THIRTY PIECES OF SILVER!

Those four words echo down through the millennia as the very definition of betrayal, although we rarely stop to think about the underlying metaphor. Our view of Judas' treachery is colored largely by the horrific character study sketched in the Gospel of John—in which he is even more than a scoundrel. He is a demon in human form, at least in John's version of this drama.

Mark stands at the other end of the dramatic spectrum with a simple scene in Chapter 14:

> And Judas Iscariot, one of the Twelve, went to the chief priests to betray Him. And when the chief priests heard this, they were glad and promised to give him money. And Judas sought how he might conveniently betray Him.

Pretty neutral and even puzzling, isn't it? In that version, we can barely glimpse the gleam and tinkle of the coins—and the authorities seem to hand over the cash almost as an afterthought.

Where's the motive here? For the full effect of the drama, we prefer Matthew's version in Chapter 26, nearly as short as Mark's version but with better stage direction:

> Then one of the Twelve, called Judas Iscariot, went to the chief priests. He said to them, "What will you give me, so that I will deliver him to you?" And they covenanted with him for 30 pieces of silver. From that time, he sought an opportunity to betray him.

In this concise version, we've at least got a motive for the betrayal: Judas' greed. And we've got a tighter sense of irony in this phrasing—by starting the little story with "Then one of the Twelve ... " This is clearly the point of the scene, isn't it? Betrayal. The "Circle of the Twelve" is now broken. And, if we've been keeping up with the entire scope of this Lenten journey, then we realize something else: Jesus already has taught us a whole lot about the metaphor of the coin! Coins embody community relationships; they are the distillation of precious human effort into a form that can flow through the larger community.

But in today's story, coins are subverted to evil. They become a symbol of utter blasphemy—selling out the Circle of Twelve! Remember how yesterday's story of the talents added to our understanding of this thing that Jesus keeps using in parables? In the talents story, a greedy slave selfishly disrupts the vital importance of passing coins throughout the community—and that slave ultimately destroys his own life. Today, in this crowning scene, we're seeing even more than mere greed, we now realize. We're witnessing the potential for the ultimate negation of life itself—right in the heart of the Circle of Twelve.

Ironically, even though this is not a coin story related by our young rabbi himself, this is our last coin story in Lent—the end of a long road for coins as teaching tools in Jesus' journey. Looming in the wings is another series of metaphors that Jesus is about to introduce in the climax of Act II. But let's not spoil those scenes just yet.

Our basic question today is this: Why on earth are we, as humans, so eager to take a masterpiece of narrative theology like Judas' betrayal—and find some way to turn this classic villain into a hero? I suspect it's because there's something in our contemporary culture that strives either to root for an underdog or to challenge authority and undermine traditional interpretations. In many cases, of course, these motivations can be terrific instincts. But, sometimes it's wise to recognize boundaries we should not cross.

Consider the strange case of Leni Riefenstahl, Adolf Hitler's favorite filmmaker, born in 1902 and only leaving the global stage in 2003 at age 101. As amazing as her transformation has been for those of us who have studied the design and impact of Nazi propaganda films, Riefenstahl desperately wanted the world to forget that she was a Nazi propagandist. She was a classic villain and yet she worked like a titan through most of her life to re-invent herself as a world-class, pioneering, feminist artist—a latter-day hero. If there were any lingering doubts about her true nature during the Nazi regime, then Steven Bach's carefully researched 2007 biography of Leni should have quashed them. In one case after another, Bach shows that her denials of culpability during the Nazi years are simply unbelievable. Since 2007, researchers have revealed even more details about the devious and deadly nature of Nazi filmmaking. Nevertheless, books remain on library shelves praising Riefenstahl as a young woman who parlayed her popularity as a beautiful, athletic young actress into a career at the pinnacle of German media. The photography she produced around the world after World War II is gorgeously seductive. As much as the world knows about her evil now, the temptation lingers to find a way to celebrate her daring.

Of course, the same urge to reform classic villains has been at work on Judas for quite a while now. In many churches, of course, Judas' role in the 2,000-year-old drama is hardly questioned. His betrayal of Jesus had to happen so that the rest of this world-changing story could unfold. Judas simply "checked off" another task on the list of prophecies that needed to be fulfilled. As most churches present the Lenten story, Judas moves a bit like a puppet across the stage. But Judas also ranks as one of the world's greatest villains, so there have been many attempts to turn his role inside out—even to somehow overturn his evil reputation. In recent years, the National Geographic Society staged a prime-time unveiling of a "Gospel of Judas," one of many ancient Gnostic documents that circulated throughout the Middle East in the centuries after Jesus' life. In the ancient world, Gnosticism was a religious movement that specialized in spiritual secrets shared by a circle of anointed insiders. It was considered a heretical break with the true faith by early Christian leaders, but was quite popular for a time and has resurfaced in new forms in our world today. Ancient Gnostics had a natural interest in trying to turn the Judas story inside out and reveal some kind of a surprising secret in his character. From their viewpoint in the Gospel of Judas, the hidden truth in this particular drama was this: Jesus secretly instructed Judas to carry out the betrayal! Judas was, as countless other villains have claimed, only following orders. Perhaps Judas wasn't so bad after all.

That particular ancient document, that Gospel of Judas, is of ongoing interest to scholars of global culture, especially those looking at the diversity of alternative voices in the ancient Middle East. But, for the vast majority of Christendom, the revelation of that document didn't change the nature of Judas' role in the real Gospels.

Could it be that Judas actually was a hero, if we only properly understand his secret motives?

To that invitation, most Christians still say firmly: No, sometimes a villain is a villain. Period.

Dipping into the First of Three Basins

PETER WANTED NO PART of the thing that happened next! And, we all should watch out *now* because, this next move tends to surprise even lifelong church-going Christians! Did you know that the universally familiar scene of the Last Supper is all but replaced in John's Gospel with a pair of basins? Today, we'll look at the first one, which shocked Peter when he first caught on to what the young rabbi was planning.

Yesterday, we pooh-poohed John's version of Judas' bribe as a bit over-the-top—too much melodrama turning Judas into such a demon that John actually robs him of some of the deeper human drama involved in betrayal. But, today, we have to salute John for his subtle narrative here, which departs from the three synoptic Gospels in one dramatic respect!

We know this story almost as well as the Last Supper, don't we? It goes like this in John 13:

> Knowing that the Father had given all things
> into his hands, and that he had come from God
> and was going to God—Jesus rose from supper
> and laid aside his garments. He took a towel and

girded himself.

After that, he poured water into a basin and began to wash the disciples' feet, and to wipe them with the towel he had wrapped around himself. Then Jesus came to Simon Peter, and Peter said to him: "Lord, are you going to wash my feet?"

Jesus said to him: "What I am doing for you, you don't understand now, but you will understand it hereafter."

Then apparently Peter could no longer contain all the conflicting emotions colliding with him as he watched his beloved teacher and master on the floor, washing feet like a servant. The problem at this point was that, as usual, Peter was so overcome by what was unfolding in front of him that the subtlety of what was unfolding in front of him had sailed right over his head. Peter had completely lost sight of the basin itself—and the way Jesus handled these symbols. Because, surely, Peter was speaking from his heart when he burst out with his next line:

Peter said to him: "You will never wash my feet!"

Jesus answered: "If I do not wash you, then you have no part in me."

Then, Simon Peter said: "Lord, then not only my feet, but also my hands and my head!"

Just in case they missed that, Jesus then drove home the lesson:

For I have given you an example and you should do as I have done to you. Truly, I say to you: The servant is not greater than his lord, nor is he who is sent greater than the one who sent him. If you understand these things, you will be happy as you do them.

So, there it is: an entirely new symbol of community, replacing the problematic symbol of the coin—a basin. This seems so obvious when we see it unfold in front of us in our journey, doesn't it?

But how easy it is to forget or misunderstand this symbol? And, soon enough, we'll see two examples of the abuse of the basin!

Now, before we triumphantly pat ourselves on the back as good servants, let's remember the American response that unfolded in the late summer of 2005 in New Orleans in the wake of Hurricane Katrina. Now, how many years have passed since the storm hit? How many thousands of Americans have been moved to travel to New Orleans to help rebuild? But, in our American response to Katrina, we have demonstrated that Jesus' example of humbling himself and handling the rough and dirty feet of poor people from the streets does not come naturally to us. In fact, most of the time, we prefer to steer as clear of rough-and-dirty people as possible.

In the days right after the storm hit, we were horrified to discover the thousands of poor people who seemed to emerge from the shadows of New Orleans into the harsh glare of national media. Even President George Bush's appointed FEMA chief expressed his shock. Who were these people who climbed up onto high ground, begging for our help? The rush to head down there, gird ourselves with towels and start washing feet was—well, verrrry sloooow. Many of the devastated homes of poor people in New Orleans are still left in ruins to this day, still waiting for help. In the summer of 2010, I traveled with my son in a 10,000-mile circle of the United Sates and, when we stopped in New Orleans, our shock at the lingering scars from Katrina led us to stop our van and walk through some of the wreckage that remained five years later! We visited New Orleans to report on the Vietnamese-American community on New Orleans' far east side that united around their Catholic church in 2005 and rebuilt their own community. These families planned and worked together to begin hauling away the mud and gunk and debris that had covered their homes. They rebuilt their church along with their homes. And, what was the immediate response to that heroic example of Christian community? Rather than celebrating their community spirit, New Orleans officials nearly destroyed what these Vietnamese-American families had rebuilt by attempting to dump the city's mountain of toxic debris from Katrina into a landfill next door to these fishermen and their families. It was only after these families led a candlelight vigil from their Catholic church into the streets to block the waste-hauling trucks that city officials finally were forced to reconsider.

As Americans, we have an enormous blind spot for the filthy, stinky plight of the poor within our communities. Yet, it's not limited to America—and it's not new. British Historian Emily Cockayne's fascinating and horrifying new book, *Hubbub: Filth, Noise and Stench in England,* makes this abundantly clear. Cockayne focuses on the utterly disgusting details of urban life in 17th and 18th century Britain in one disturbing chapter after another. If you were poor in Britain, as most people were in that era, can you imagine walking through an open sewer on your way to work? Then, once you're there, choking all day long on a haze of smoke and other odors? And, when you're thirsty, sipping diseased water?

No wonder the rich disdained the poor, we quickly conclude. And, after reading a few chapters of her book, it's a wonder that our ancestors lived to produce future generations! Apparently, people have the capacity to get used to almost anything. Unless—*unless* someone does something as dramatic as Jesus did, when he hauled out a simple basin, filled it with water and approached those dirty feet. I suspect a whole lot of us would have reacted as Peter did. We don't want our spiritual master and friend to bruise his knees on the floor and handle—our feet! But Jesus is as deadly serious about this symbol as he was in explaining how coins were to be used. He wanted his followers to see that community thrives on human interaction and good community thrives on the compassionate flow of human contact.

"If I do not wash you, then you have no part in me."

That's as uncompromising as Jesus' story about the slaves and the talents. He has no patience, at this point in our journey, for those who try to turn away from the dirty, smelly and downright uncomfortable details of true compassion.

Sister Aimee Empties and Tries to Refill the Bowl

IN OUR LENTEN REFLECTIONS down through the years, most of us probably have overlooked this middle bowl. We all know about the basin used in the washing of the feet—and we can guess at the third bowl that lies ahead of us. But this second one? It's easy to miss. So, let's slow down the action for a moment, shall we, and regard it carefully? Three of the four Gospels place a second bowl center stage at this point in our journey. And, it's quite a striking thing, once we recognize the background—that our Lenten journey includes three bowls and all of them are things that make us think of the dynamics of community. Luke's is the Gospel that ignores this particular piece. He simply has Jesus' prediction of betrayal occur at a meal, so presumably a bowl is center stage, but Luke doesn't point it out explicitly.

In Matthew 26, the new bowl appears like this:

> When the evening came, he sat down with the
> twelve. As they ate, he said: "Truly, I tell you that

one of you shall betray me."
And they were exceedingly sorrowful and began,
every one of them, to say to him: "Lord, is it I?"
And he answered: "One who dips his hand with
me into this dish will betray me."

Now, it's quite understandable that we've often overlooked the bowl sitting right there in front of us—because the preceding line, "Lord is it I?" (or other translations of that line), are among the most memorable words in 2,000 years of the world's sacred texts. In Mark, there may be a little more specificity in the scene. Jesus says: "It is one of the twelve who dips with me in this dish." However, translations vary and often use identical wording in both Mark and Matthew.

Ultimately it falls to John, bent on heightening the whole drama around Judas, who deftly crafts the story into a scene worthy of a Hitchcock film. As John writes it, Jesus responded to calls for him to identify his betrayer with a chilling line that dramatically described what he was about to do with the common bowl. Jesus apparently held up a piece of bread and said that his betrayer "is the one to whom I shall give this bread, when I have dipped it." Who could take a breath in the next moment in that scene?

All things considered, these are very similar traditions—suggesting that the betrayal prediction was closely associated with the intimacy of a meal. And, frankly, doesn't it make our skin crawl to think of the villain's hands mingling with all the rest of Jesus' followers as everyone reaches into the common bowl? We may have thought it was uncomfortable when coins, as a symbol of community, were used as tools of betrayal. But literally feeling the warm stroke of a villain's hand as we reach for our next bite of supper? Ooooof! That's gut-wrenching.

Then, the larger question becomes: What do we owe to the community in the common bowl we share? What do we put into the bowl and what do we take out? And once we've agreed to share a bowl, do we stop to think how devastating a betrayal of this intimacy might become?

In recent years, Americans have heard a lot about a famous evangelist who both filled the bowl—and abused the intimacy of the bowl. Then, historians would argue, she tried in the final years of her life to restore the bowl and all the relationships around the table. Her name was Sister Aimee Semple McPherson, and historian Matthew Avery Sutton's fascinating biography was made into an hour-long PBS documentary in the American Experience series. The film later was released on DVD and the renewed interest in Sister Aimee sparked further coverage of her life.

Born in 1890, Sister Aimee was at such an impressionable age at the dawn of the American Pentecostal movement that she was swept up in its spiritual fire. With no real preparation, she and her young husband, Robert Semple, headed into the Asian mission field, where he was dead within months of preventable illness.

Returning to the U.S., Sister Aimee still had the revivalist fire running through her veins. She married grocery clerk Harold McPherson, who wanted her to settle down with him and raise a family. But that wasn't her vocation. Even though this was an era when demeaning newspaper reporters would tell their readers that the idea of a woman evangelist was as bizarre as watching a trained dog dance the waltz on its hind legs—she hit the road with her mother and two children in tow.

There were several innovations that make Sister Aimee a spiritual pioneer who we can truly say was filling up the Christian bowl with something remarkably nourishing. First, she was unstoppable in her quest to break gender barriers in religious leadership, no matter the mud that her critics might toss her way.

Second, she was decades ahead of Billy Graham in breaking racial barriers in nationwide revival tours. In 1918, Sutton reports, she began a revival in Key West, welcoming both black and white residents of the island. When she discovered that black families felt unsafe coming to the white part of the island, she moved her traveling evangelistic show to a black neighborhood. Aimee explained the move this way: "God so definitely called us that we could not hesitate." And, when many whites felt moved to at least temporarily abandon their racial barriers to continue attending her services, she shouted, "Glory! All walls of prejudice are breaking down!"

Finally, Sister Aimee was a performance artist of incredible daring who developed a series of "Illustrated Sermons," which amounted to full-scale stage shows based on biblical stories. She also paved the way for the kind of elaborately produced, seeker-friendly services that pack America's biggest megachurches to this day.

Detroit reporter Rex G. White, covering a 1929 appearance by Sister Aimee at the Masonic Temple, reported on the front page that he'd seen what he thought were the best evangelists of the day, including Billy Sunday in his prime—but those spiritual showmen couldn't hold a candle to Sister Aimee's use of costumes, choreography, stage settings, lighting effects and a whole series of dramatic sketches woven through her revival shows.

At one point, White wrote: a "dozen or more pretty girls in pink and rose-colored capes did a left entrance and took the center of the stage, when the house lights were dimmed and baby spots with yellow and rose rays played on the leading figure, when 'Onward Christian Soldiers' was syncopated and done with variations on two grand pianos by young ladies in uniform, when a banked mixed chorus performed choreography with handkerchiefs to a hymn played in waltz time, when the house was asked to join in singing, 'Aloha' ... the leading lady appeared in sparkling blond curls ... done up à la Mary Pickford in many curls. She was dressed in white silk with a long skirt and a cape that gave the effect of a Christmas-card angel when she waved her arms. A white-covered Bible completed the costume."

After such dramatic effects, White wrote, she "left the observer wondering if the proceedings were opera with religious leanings or religion with operatic leanings."

Of course, Sister Aimee is remembered today (and surely the PBS documentary wouldn't have been made without this chapter of her life), because of all she grabbed back out of the common bowl in the middle years of her life. Smitten with Hollywood's glittering wealth and fame, she began backsliding on her commitment to racial equality—and began ushering any new black converts away from her altar calls to separate "colored" congregations in other parts of Los Angeles. She began to collect wealthy friends, extravagant cars—and eventually in 1926 she staged a six-week getaway that she tried to pass off as a kidnapping. She spent more time on the nation's front pages that year than virtually anyone else in the U.S. A criminal trial for fraud followed and, according to Sutton, these years represented a spiritual wilderness for the strong-willed Sister Aimee.

What's amazing about her story, Sutton reports, is that she did turn her life around in her remaining years after the shock of the trial. She called black evangelists to join her at her Angelus Temple in Los Angeles and, by the time she passed through Detroit in 1929 and visited New Baltimore, Michigan, in 1933—she was trying to rekindle the fire that had fueled her initial love affair with millions of Americans.

She remained an unrepentant Fundamentalist throughout her life and her legacy is checkered at best, but Sutton's book argues that Sister Aimee almost single-handedly pulled the American Pentecostal movement into the mainstream of American life. She handed down many of Pentecostalism's most powerful religious techniques to her successors—spiritual skills that evangelists continue to pull out of the common bowl decades after her death in 1944.

Not bad for a farm girl from Ontario who had little but her raw religious instincts about how to form spiritual connections as she barnstormed America and left her first two husbands behind in her dust.

For some years, like the villain in our Lenten journey today, she did betray the common bowl—but there's a reassuring sense of redemption in the way that, once she was confronted with her villainy, she worked to refill that bowl for the rest of us.

Breaking Bread with a Loving French Chef

*As they were eating, Jesus took bread, and
blessed it, and broke it, and gave it to the
disciples, and said, "Take, eat; this is my body."*

—Matthew 26:26

*Warning Americans in the late 1980s that they should
get over their rising anxieties about food—the great
culinary teacher described the growing problem in
these simple yet spiritual terms: "The dinner table
is becoming a trap rather than a pleasure!"*

—From Laura Shapiro's biography, *Julia Child*

TODAY, WE SAY: "THANK heavens" for the Public Broadcasting Service's tireless efforts to expand our understanding of the world. That's because, at this point in our journey with Jesus, we're in need of considerable help to reflect on one of the most difficult things in the concluding scene of Act II. Of course, we're talking about bread.

Why is bread such a tough thing to experience in a fresh way? Well, for weeks now, we've experienced Jesus' efforts to awaken our senses, our minds and our hearts to the all-too-common stuff of life. Eventually, the Gospels tell us, Jesus reached for bread—a symbol that's so central to daily life and our spiritual heritage that it's almost impossible to jolt ourselves into a fresh awareness of it.

Then, there is Laura Shapiro's intriguing biography of legendary PBS cooking-show pioneer Julia Child, who passed away in 2004. Spiritual light bulbs begin flashing soon after we open up Shapiro's account of Child's innovations. She was, after all, the woman who transformed TV cooking shows in the early 1960s from dull lessons in home economics to mass entertainment—and, as a result, taught Americans to think of food, cooking and their dinner tables in a whole new way.

Shapiro argues that the key to Julia Child's beloved status with millions of Americans was Child's complete honesty in her zest for life, which conveyed far more than cooking techniques to her audience. Child's real vocation was teaching Americans an honest, daily discipline for their relationship to food and family. That's exactly how director Norah Ephron and actress Meryl Streep brought Child to life in the 2009 hit comedy *Julie & Julia*—as straight-forward as a bulldozer in her mission to reconnect the wider world with traditions of good eating.

Do you recall watching Julia Child's shows? If so, you'll remember how much she loved food. Here's what Shapiro writes about Child's personal relationship to food: "Julia Child loved handling food. She loved slathering great gobs of butter around a pan with her bare hand … When she explained the different cuts of beef on her legendary public television series, she used her own body as the butcher's chart, twisting to display her back or side as if to make clear the intimate relationship between the cook and the meat."

These are fascinating biographical notes to read in parallel with our scripture passage today, aren't they? Note how Shapiro sums up Child's overall message to her viewers over her television table: "Use all your senses, all the time, Julia instructed. Take pains with

the work; do it carefully. Relish the details. Enjoy your hunger.
And remember why you're there."
All our senses?
We're trying our best to do that each day in this unusual
Lenten pilgrimage, aren't we?
Take pains with the work?
Mindfulness is our method here, isn't it?
Relish the details?
Certainly!
Enjoy your hunger?
A timeless Lenten lesson.
And—remember?
Yes, remember.

Jesus' Two Cups and Pouring Ourselves into the World

TWO CUPS! TWO CUPS held high. At this point in our Lenten journey, envision a curtain falling on Act II of our drama—and these tantalizing symbols of raised cups linking the second and third acts of our narrative. Jesus raises one cup in a startling crescendo in the Last Supper. Later, he passionately lifts the metaphor of a cup in prayer as he contemplates pouring out his life in a sacrificial act.

Surely, it is time to explicitly raise a question that, perhaps, we've been subtly asking ourselves throughout all the weeks of this journey: Where in this story do you find your salvation?

The question is posed this way, because a host of readers have joined our Lenten journey from a wide range of religious traditions. As companions in this journey, we may find signs of our salvation in a broad array of things and spiritual insights we've gleaned along our journey. As we move into the final acts of our story, we're finding things like these cups hugely magnified—reverberating with timeless spiritual lessons and echoing all kinds of associations with Jesus' teachings.

So, where in this weeks-long drama do you find your salvation? It wasn't an easy question then and it isn't now. Jesus' followers certainly were all over the spiritual map about what was unfolding in their midst. Frankly, Jesus' words and actions weren't as crystal clear as some preachers would have us believe. In the midst of Jesus' dramatic prayer in John's 17th chapter, he speaks to God and declares that the overall purpose of this journey is: "As You have sent me into the world, I have sent them into the world."

Hearing this kind of prayer come from Jesus' lips, his followers must have been shaking their heads just a little bit: What? The point of this journey is that we're preparing ourselves for—another journey? Jesus certainly seems to indicate that the first cup holds that promise of further travels. In Matthew 26, we read:

> Jesus took the cup, and gave thanks, and gave
> it to them, saying: "Drink all of it; for this is my
> blood of the new testament, which is shed for
> many for the remission of sins. But I say to you,
> I will not drink further of this fruit of the vine,
> until that day when I drink it new with you in
> my Father's kingdom."

Mark's version is virtually identical. Luke is similar, although Luke connects the words over the cup with a specific prediction by Jesus about his looming betrayal and links the betrayal to the spilling of blood from the cup. If we're looking for crystal clear instruction, this famous scene doesn't exactly etch Jesus' meaning with a diamond edge. In fact, we may have overlooked the fact that—for all of the spiritual power of this historic gesture, the lifting of the first cup never appears in John's Gospel! Then, in John's Act III, there's no second cup, either. John's version of the drama describes a far more decisive and self-assured Jesus than the Jesus depicted in these scenes in the three synoptic Gospels.

Do you recall the scene in the garden in the three earlier Gospels? They all cast Jesus as praying in agony. Matthew and Mark say that Jesus "threw himself on the ground." The King James Version painfully says that Jesus "fell on his face." Most ancient versions of Luke say that Jesus sweat blood as he prayed. As printed in our modern Bibles, Jesus' lines are easy to misunderstand. The lines are recalled almost identically in all three synoptic Gospels: "O my Father, if it is possible, let this cup pass from me; nevertheless, not what I wish, but as You will."

There's a whole cosmos of agony in that semicolon. Perhaps Bibles should be designed with an ocean of suspenseful "white space" between the first and second halves of that line.

After these weeks of considering the many things Jesus has shown us, we should not be surprised that Jesus didn't sugar-coat what was unfolding. That was never his style. At this point in our journey, facing this challenge of describing how his own life is being poured out for the world, Jesus frames his description with a strikingly honest glimpse of the violence that millions in our world experience every day.

The world is an extremely dangerous place and violent tragedies will continue to befall people we love, Jesus warns, especially in the 15th and 16th chapters of John's version of this scene. Our choice, Jesus says, is how we choose to pour out our lives. John's 16th chapter ends with these powerful words from Jesus: "These things I have told you, so that in me you might find peace. In the world, you shall have tribulation. But, be of good cheer, for I have overcome the world."

Wherever you find your salvation in our unfolding journey, this much is clear: The world continues to bleed, just as Jesus predicted it would. While writing this book, I searched for fresh ways to describe these scenes that most Christians have known all their lives. So, I asked a group of teen-agers to talk about these metaphors of the two cups. First, I asked them: Where do you see the world bleeding today?

"Iraq," said one.

"Haiti," said another.

"In wars and genocides in places like Africa and poor parts of Asia."

"Sometimes," said a boy, "when I close my eyes and think of the wars in Iraq and Afghanistan, what I see is a chaotic square, crowded with people running everywhere and shooting each other."

"There is screaming, but much of it is in silence," said one eloquent student.

There was a pause. Then, one student said, "When we think of people bleeding in our world today, I think of homeless people who sleep in our alleys. You know there are some right near our church?"

Nearby, a boy was jotting notes on a piece of paper as he listened to the others. He wrote this question: "Are people bleeding everywhere in our world?"

Now, re-read Jesus' words: "These things I have told you, so that in me you might find peace. In the world, you shall have tribulation. But, be of good cheer, for I have overcome the world." If you don't recall that long sequence in John 15 to 17, check it out. The spiritual parallels are obvious with what this group of high school students were saying.

"What's so hard about all of this," said one boy, "is that it's so confusing. I went to Haiti with my family when I was little. And we saw so many sick people there. Some of them didn't know why they were sick; they didn't know where to go for help; and then they came to us for help. There were so many of them who needed help."

The parallels with Jesus' instructions to his followers are haunting, aren't they? Jesus said, "As You have sent me into the world, I have sent them into the world."

And then, there's that second cup! Do we ask that it be removed—or do we accept it? Among the students, I asked this second question: "If you could choose right now—and tell us whatever comes to the front of your mind first—what would you choose to pour your life into?"

Their answers were honest: "Fun in my life," one boy answered.

And a girl said, "Horses, I already spend a lot of time with horses and nothing can dampen my desire to keep coming back to this."

That's a sincere slice of real life, isn't it? People are people and, everywhere in the world, we simply want to enjoy our lives—a stark contrast from the first question. If we can choose to pour out our lives, none of us wants to do it in the form of losing life's blood. We want to pour ourselves into something that gives us joy. These answers truly came from budding gospel writers in the group—who wanted to share the good news of their joy for life with others.

"I want to write so that I could connect with anyone who reads what I write," said one student. "I want anyone who reads what I write to see what I am seeing."

Another shared this sense of vocation: "What I really would love to pour my life into is writing—writing everything: poetry, short stories and novels. I'd even like to be a librarian so I could study writings and write myself."

These are encouraging words to hear. Millions of hearts around the world are bursting with such aspirations—fun, the enjoyment of animals, reading, writing, connecting with the larger world.

And, then, this also came from a girl in the group: "I'd like to pour myself into listening to people and helping them—helping them try to look at the world from other angles." And the goal of all of this, she said, was to make "friends," and to pour herself out "in love."

And, truly we say: That was the lesson of the two cups 2,000 years ago. And so it is in hopeful hearts around the world—to this very day.

Jesus and a Shakespearean Tale of Two Swords

YESTERDAY, WE FOUND A connection between two cups drawing us into the high drama of Act III in our Lenten journey. Today, we find another pair of things—two swords—linking the fierce scene of Jesus' arrest by soldiers back to Jesus' instructions to his followers just a little earlier in our adventure. It's an anachronism to say that we're at a truly Shakespearean moment in our drama. All around us, things that we have invested with timeless spiritual significance are arrayed along our Lenten road. All of the complex threads in our drama now are pulling us toward a crescendo. The truth is that many centuries later, in his greatest masterpieces, Shakespeare was truly biblical in his dramatic sensibility.

Here's the first and most fearsome sword at hand today: Jesus has completed his prayers in the garden on the Mount of Olives, across the valley from the Holy City, his betrayal is at hand, the soldiers are closing in and Luke tells us in Chapter 22:

> When those who were around him saw what
> was happening, they said to him: "Lord, shall we

strike with the sword?" And one of them struck
the servant of the high priest, and cut off his
right ear.
Jesus answered: "Stop this now." And he touched
the ear and healed the man.
Then, Jesus said to the chief priests, the captains
of the Temple, and the elders who had come to
get him: "Have you come out with these swords
and wooden staves as if coming to capture a
thief?"

Of course, they had! But, if we assume that this is evidence
of Jesus' non-violent opposition to carrying weaponry, then we've
completely missed a key, but troubling scene, just a little earlier
in the same Chapter 22 of Luke. Most of us probably have overlooked that first sword scene in our past journeys through Lent.
It's a scene set just prior to Jesus' prayers on the Mount of Olives
and it's a pragmatic instruction by our young rabbi to his followers.

Jesus said to them: "When I sent you without
purse, a bag and shoes, did you lack anything?"
And they said: "Nothing."

In this instruction, Jesus is referring even further back to his
teaching in Luke's Chapters 9 and 10 as he first sent out his followers "to proclaim the kingdom of God and to heal." Now, in
Chapter 22, Jesus is ripping up his earlier rulebook to prepare for
a tough new era in ministry. Jesus' fresh instruction goes like this:

"But now, whoever has a purse, take it, and likewise a bag. And, he who has no sword let him
sell his garment—and buy one. For I say to you
that it is written and still must be accomplished
in my life: 'And he was ranked among the law
breakers.' For these things concerning me must
all pass."
His followers immediately produced some
swords that they could carry with them—and

Luke reports that Jesus looked over the little arsenal and told his followers, "It is enough."

Well, at first glance, there's a very practical side to this often-overlooked passage. It handily explains why there's a sword flashing in the garden scene. After all, the rabbi had just told his followers to have swords ready! This was such an important part of his instruction that, if they hadn't owned swords already, he wanted them to sell their clothes and purchase swords. But this whole thing seems a bit bizarre. After all, leaping ahead to the Acts of the Apostles, how many times do you recall Jesus' followers pulling out swords and mixing it up with enemies in that epic story of the early church? Can't think of a single sword fight in Acts, right? So, what's the deal with all these swords in Luke 22?

Well, one echo here harks back to that strange instruction by our young rabbi, earlier in our journey, about the need to stay savvy as snakes. If you've forgotten Chapter 19, then take a moment to look back.

But, here's another way to think about the swords. I have been surprised in recent years by the number of religiously minded reviewers who have praised the 2007 Oscar winner as Best Foreign Language Film: *The Lives of Others*, set in East Germany during the Cold War. Just as in Luke 22, the film explores dueling swords, at least in a figurative sense, in a drama of Shakespearean proportions.

Most of the film is set in a bleak East German high-rise housing complex. In an apartment on a lower floor in the building, a couple of young lovers reside in a setting of music, literature, art and warm hues in nearly every scene. The man is a playwright and classical pianist; the woman is a famous actress on the East German stage. However, high above them, perched just under the building's rafters in a bleak, blue-gray loft populated only by stacks of electronic surveillance gear, sits a grim-faced agent of the secret police, determined to catch the young couple in some honest moment of criticism of their Orwellian government. If he captures even a hint of a seditious comment, he can destroy their lives with a flick of a button on his recording devices. Quite literally, we watch as the agent's secret microphones descend down through the walls into the couple's apartment like razor-sharp swords just waiting there to destroy them. But there is a second set of swords that rise from the couple's apartment. These swords take the form of the arousing power of their music, their poetry and the signs of their compassionate love for each other and for others in their inner circle of friends.

Captain Wiesler, the secret agent in the attic, has circumscribed his own life so tightly that, once he zips himself into his tight, silver-colored coat and dedicates himself fully to his mission, he seems almost like a sword himself. What's amazing is that, before we know it, he's so intrigued by a collection of short stories that he hears the young couple discuss in the apartment below that he sneaks downstairs when they are away—and steals it. The next thing we know, he's curled up reading—probably the first literature he has encountered in decades. Soon, the persuasive tip of a literary sword from the couple far below him has nicked his steely outer shell.

And that's not all. A member of the couple's inner circle, an elderly writer who served as the young playwright's most beloved mentor, tragically dies after years of persecution from the secret police. After the death of this man, the younger writer consoles himself by playing classics on his piano so soulfully that he whispers to the actress, "At hearing such music, anyone who has a soul must weep."

The camera rises from this scene, as if slicing through all the floors between their apartment and the surveillance loft—and we find the tightly zipped agent, despite his stiff resolve, beginning to weep.

Soon, the agent begins to risk his own life to protect his targets in small ways. Later, he defends them in larger and larger ways, until he is trading his own future for his selfless love of this young couple. It's a heart-rending transformation to watch over the film's two hours.

But, as in our Lenten journey with the young rabbi, there are larger forces at work in this Soviet-era imperial world. Powerful socialist bosses begin to throw their deadly weight into this fragile trio of lives co-existing in the high-rise apartment.

Of course, in our Gospel accounts, the Roman Empire looms like a bird of prey high above our little band of companions. Whose sword will prevail? That's the question in closing scenes of *The Lives of Others* and in closing chapters of our Lenten journey, as well.

A Third Basin, Hannah Arendt and Banality of Evil

WE FIND OURSELVES SO deep in the heart of Lent that we might think of it as Act III in this timeless drama. We're beginning to explore some of the "final things" in our journey; and we're discovering a remarkable resonance arising from our accumulation of experiences and reflections. The spiritual impact of Jesus' method—and the narrative tradition that flows from his style of teaching—begins to echo like rolling thunder.

Today, we're suddenly face to face with: a *third* basin. We've now built a powerful triptych of these symbols of community—and betrayal when the basins are misused. In Chapter 28 of our Lenten story, we watched as Jesus took the first basin, wrapped a towel around his hips and began washing his followers' dirty feet. Then, in Chapter 29 of our series, we were shocked to recall how even members of Jesus' inner circle were tempted to abuse the intimacy of a shared bowl, the second basin.

Now, there's this third basin. Surely, you recall this famous scene: Jesus is caught in the grip of Roman imperial authority and we find figures like Pontius Pilate, the Roman governor of the

Province of Judea, processing his case through the legal system of that era. This was a turbulent time in Middle Eastern history. Bible scholars like Marcus Borg and John Dominic Crossan argue persuasively that Jesus, most likely, was fed through the cruelly efficient imperial system with other trouble makers who had been swept up by the Roman authorities—pretty much like cattle through a chute at a slaughterhouse. It's tempting, given the enormous spiritual significance we now see in Jesus' life, to cast these scenes in Jerusalem as titanic confrontations of Spirit and Empire. And, while we certainly do agree that these things were filled with overwhelming meaning for humanity—the truth of what actually unfolded on the ground in Jerusalem 2,000 years ago probably was far closer to what German political theorist Hannah Arendt described as "the Banality of Evil."

Arendt, who died in 1975, was born in 1906 in what is now Germany and managed to escape the Holocaust by fleeing to the United States with her family. Her complex and sometimes controversial life was dominated by 20th-century questions about freedom, moral responsibility, the global failure embodied in the Holocaust and the nature of possible political action that might overcome such catastrophes in the future. In 1961 and 1962, she wrote in *The New Yorker* about the trial of Nazi war criminal Adolf Eichmann, who had been captured in Argentina and was carried to Israel for these historic hearings that eventually resulted in his execution. Afterward, she published her influential book, *Eichmann in Jerusalem: A Report on the Banality of Evil*. In the book, Arendt argued that Eichmann was not a monster and showed no signs of mental illness. In fact, he was a typical bureaucrat in an imperial system who morally justified his role in organizing the Final Solution as if it was merely a noble example of patriotic work by a loyal civil servant.

Eichmann himself argued in court that he had no moral responsibility that should be described as a crime, since he was working in the service of a far larger system and that decisions governing his actions were made at levels far above him. His only moral duty was to follow orders, he argued. He was able to carry out his work with tragic efficiency, Arendt concluded, because he knitted around himself a tapestry of what Arendt called *Amtssprache,* or "officialese." This insular approach to the world—hemmed in by officialese until people actually believe that they have no moral responsibility to the larger community—was the fatal flaw in so many political systems around the world, Arendt argued. Too many systems encourage this Banality of Evil.

Of course, in Eichmann, we're talking about a world-class war criminal responsible for millions of deaths—but we can see that this principle Arendt describes is powerfully played out in countless other lives, as well, if we just stop to think about it. Go back and read the parts in which Pilate is cast in the four Gospels. The basin actually appears only by implication in Matthew's 27th chapter:

> When Pilate saw that he could do nothing, and
> a tumult was rising in the crowd, he took water
> and washed his hands in front of the multitude,
> saying, "I am innocent of the blood of this just
> person!"

This famous hand-washing scene—so often depicted with pitcher, basin and towel dramatically displayed before a nearly out-of-control crowd—winds up ironically echoing Jesus' own earlier washing scene in this drama. Oddly, though, considering its dramatic power and enduring popularity in people's memories—the Pilate hand-washing doesn't appear in the other three Gospels.

Pause for a moment in reflection on this amazing thing: this basin. Think about the lines Pilate delivers over the basin. This is classic *Amtssprache,* isn't it? "I am innocent of the blood of this just person!" Listen to the echoes. Hear them? Even now?

Pick up major U.S. newspapers or news magazines and flip through news stories around the world. You'll find stories about corruption as a commonly accepted condition of life in areas of Africa and Asia. And, closer to home? You'll find headlines about abuse in U.S.-run prisons, or white-collar crimes on Wall Street, or American veterans suffering with sub-standard medical care—all conditions that the professionals in charge somehow manage to overlook until public outrage begins to boil.

The Banality of Evil—perhaps recast as the Public Basin of Evil—is a powerful metaphor for this spiritual evil. Unfortunately, it's yet another reminder that our Lenten journey is no less than timeless, no less than true.

Kindness of Strangers and Danger of Betrayal

Then, the King will say to those on his right hand: Come, you who are blessed of my Father, inherit the kingdom prepared for you from the foundation of the world. For I was hungry, and you gave me meat; I was thirsty, and you gave me drink: I was a stranger, and you took me in.

—Jesus talking to his followers in Matthew 25

"IS THERE ANY HOPE for congregations?" It's a question I hear when I visit houses of worship, coast to coast. The truth is, the transformation in our religious institutions is as historic as the turbulence reshaping traditional news media and publishing. The sad truth is that thousands of congregations won't survive. Surviving congregations will be those where people truly appreciate the spiritual treasures and relationships they find there, rather than merely keeping the doors open as a kind of local shrine or clubhouse. What do we mean by "spiritual treasures"? Well, one of the most valuable gems is right there in Matthew 25. In fact, it's a theme that concerned Jesus throughout his entire life: *strangers.* One major difference between growing and dwindling congregations is the way they treat strangers, so it is worth spending a day on this very important thing.

In fact, it doesn't overstate the Gospel message to say: Our own hope depends on how well we recognize and relate to strangers. If we truly accept God's grace in our own lives, and truly understand Jesus' message, then our lives must extend past our own comfortable cubicles to connect with all of the other people who make up this vast kingdom. And, yes, if you're following our journey closely, we're echoing Chapter 25 here.

Just think about the phrase, "the kindness of strangers," the famous Tennessee Williams phrase from *Streetcar Named Desire*, dripping with bitter irony as the tarnished Southern belle Blanche DuBois drawls, "I have always depended on the kindness of strangers." Understanding Blanche's checkered past, the hair stands up on the back of our necks as she delivers her trademark line. Since *Streetcar*, the phrase signals precisely the opposite of kindness when it is repeated in literature and the arts—a signal that the strangers we're about to encounter are anything but kind. It took a *New Yorker* journalist, a courageous photographer and then an American artist living in Barcelona to show us that one of the most indelible scars from the long-running war in Iraq is our thoughtless treatment of strangers. Now that U.S. forces have officially left Iraq, this tragedy continues to unfold. Countless Iraqi men and women who aided American forces—strangers who became our friends and allies—are now left to persecution and in many cases death. Journalist George Packer wrote a powerful *New Yorker* magazine piece about the problem, headlined:

"BETRAYED: The Iraqis who trusted Americans the most"

If you can't recall Packer's long story, you may recall seeing the photographs that appeared with it, including a huge Christoph Bangert photograph displayed dead center in the middle of Packer's story. Bangert's photo showed an ordinary, middle-aged man—a guy who looks a lot like one of our co-workers, neighbors or fellow parishioners perhaps—dressed in khakis and a neat button-down dress shirt. But, wait! As viewers examined that photo, it was obvious that something was wrong with this man! He was lying on his side. We wondered: Perhaps he fell down? There was a black cord wrapped around his wrists. And, wait! Why couldn't we see his head in the shadows at the side of this photograph? What was wrong with this man—this stranger with the clothing and the overall appearance of a friend? Well, the problem was: He was dead.

This poor man was just one of the countless men and women executed in sectarian attacks and dumped along Baghdad roads. Bangert's caption tells us that, like many people found this way in Baghdad, it was impossible for Iraqi authorities to identify him. Packer reported that the people most likely to meet such an end are the Iraqis who helped Americans during the war. We welcomed these strangers in our midst, but Packer reports that, as violence escalated in recent years, we wound up betraying virtually everyone with whom we made contact by simply leaving them to fend for themselves with no provision for their safety.

Such a truth, complete with the photograph, was so overwhelming that it shocked compassionate men and women around the world. Among those indelibly marked by the "gruesome and appalling" photo was artist Frank Plant, who lives and works in Barcelona. Plant wrote, "This image haunted me and made me think about the liberties that we so often take for granted without having to fear that someone was going to drag us out of the house in the middle of the night off to the local garbage dump for a bullet in the back of the head." He turned the image into one of his iconic wire-frame sculptures, which he displayed both among his other works and posted online to haunt the rest of the world with this truth.

The truth is that, as we reach Holy Week, the theme of the stranger echoes from the Way of the Cross to post-resurrection appearances, doesn't it?

Do you realize that the Gospel verdict is 3-to-1 that Jesus did not carry his own cross? Only John, who goes out of his way in his Gospel to emphasize Jesus' stark sacrificial act, describes Jesus as carrying the cross himself. All three other Gospels say that it was a complete stranger who was forced by the Romans to carry the cross for Jesus. Although artists have waffled on this 3-to-1 verdict down through the centuries—often depicting someone lending Jesus a hand with the cross—please, read the Gospels for yourself. They say that a complete stranger carried the cross—period. His name was Simon and he was from Cyrene in what is now Libya in northern Africa. Perhaps he was black; perhaps he was a Jewish man from the large Jewish community in Cyrene. We don't know for sure. What we do know is that he was grabbed out of the crowd by the soldiers. Mark and Matthew say the Romans "compelled" Simon to do this. Luke says they "seized" him. This sounds like brutal handling for a stranger in town—yet, his appearance on the scene suddenly focused history's spotlight upon him and this one act in his life defined him in a powerful way. He was identified by the early church and his brief moment on the vast stage of the Bible has been retold for 2,000 years.

Imagine that! Here is a stranger who, to this day, millions envy for his proximity to Jesus at a key turning point in Jesus' life. And, what about the other bit players who also are about to step onto the stage? There are two men on crosses next to Jesus' cross—and one of them suddenly finds himself welcomed by Jesus in a way that likely makes the rest of us a little jealous. Then, there's Joseph of Arimathea, another bit player who suddenly shows up playing a major role in the drama—caring for the burial of Jesus' body. Later legends claim that Joseph was honored as the keeper of the Holy Grail after Jesus' death.

Of course, the roadway extends beyond the crucifixion, doesn't it? And surely we recall the mysterious stranger who showed up on that post-crucifixion roadway? Even Jesus' closest friends did not recognize that stranger at first. Truly, this is a week when we're likely to encounter more than our normal share of strangers. How alert will we be to their presence? Truly, our own hopes may be bound up in how well we welcome them.

Perhaps it is *our* kindness that matters even more than theirs.

Finally Confronting the Naked Truth

Then, Job arose, and tore his cloak, and shaved his head, and fell down upon the ground—and worshiped. Job said: "Naked, I came from my mother's womb—and naked shall I leave this life. The Lord gave, and the Lord has taken away. Blessed be the name of the lord."

—from Job 1:20-21

IN HALF A CENTURY of listening to sermons, I can't recall even a single little homily preached on the next remarkable thing in our journey: nakedness.

Perhaps this is because there's so much other material to cover in Holy Week sermons about sacrifice and salvation that no one has time for such a potentially disturbing topic as the spiritual nature of nudity in the Lenten narrative. But, it is true that the 10th Station of the Cross, observed by more than a billion Christians around the world, is the Stripping of Jesus by the Romans preparing to crucify him. And many artists down through the centuries, even many modern artists, have visually meditated on this theme in rendering the Stations.

I'm not naïve. I understand that it's tough to come to terms with the almost overwhelming number of references to nudity in the final scenes of the Gospel accounts. No wonder it's routinely and wisely ignored by preachers as a disconcerting choice for the crowds of strangers who show up in Holy Week, especially at Easter with their children expectantly arrayed in new holiday clothes, all set for the family photos at the Easter dinner that's really the highlight of the day. In Easter services, it's enough to cover the basic Good News in the scant time allotted for sermons.

But the nudity at this point in our Lenten journey was obviously calculated by Gospel writers to shock us, so it is certainly worth exploring today. What's fascinating 2,000 years after Jesus walked the road to Jerusalem is finding his name invoked in a *Wired* magazine cover story on nakedness, also known as "transparency" in the business world. Imagine that! Jesus' name appeared in huge type in *Wired*, cast as an expert source on the need to strip ourselves bare as an ultimate symbol of honesty. However, before we jump to *Wired*, let's review what we're talking about in the Gospel accounts—because (other than the 10th Station of the Cross) this is material that's routinely overlooked in our pulpits.

Matthew, Mark and John are the chief Gospel writers who hammer home this visual metaphor. Mark starts earliest, back at the scene in the Garden on the Mount of Olives when Jesus is praying, then is arrested and hauled away in a shocking scene of betrayal and violence. In Mark's 14th chapter, Mark describes Jesus' followers scrambling away before they are arrested, too:

> His followers all abandoned him and fled. Also following him was a certain young man who wore only a linen cloth. When they laid hold of his cloak and tried to capture him, he left the linen cloth behind and fled from them naked.

Perhaps this is historical detail—the arrest in the Garden was so shattering to Jesus' followers that at least one man fled the scene naked, presumably his body scratched and bleeding from the rocks and shadowy olive branches that surely would have injured him in his nighttime flight. Or, perhaps this scene is a narrative foreshadowing of what's about to happen to Jesus himself—stripped by the Roman soldiers.

In Matthew's 27th chapter, the attention to such detail seems to be almost a poetic refrain. During the soldiers' torture and mocking of Jesus, Matthew reports, they stripped him of his clothes, not once—but twice. Then, in verse 35, they stripped him a third time in the crucifixion process before gambling for his garments.

John extends the detail even beyond the crucifixion and resurrection into the appearance stories at the end of his Gospel! Clearly, there's a point to all of this explicit nudity, so carefully noted and repeated by these writers. John's final nude scene is in Chapter 21 as some of the disciples, after the loss of Jesus, are out fishing in the Sea of Tiberias. They spot a man standing on the beach; the man calls out to them across the water—and they realize that it's Jesus! John reports:

> Then, the disciple whom Jesus loved turned to Peter and said: "It is the Lord." And, when Simon Peter heard that it was the Lord, he pulled a fisherman's cloak around him, for he was naked, and threw himself into the sea. The other disciples came to shore in the ship; for they were not far from land, dragging the net with fishes.

What is the point to all of this—this lack of clothing? Well, we couldn't put it any better than *Wired* magazine—in a special issue with a tricky double-cover showing a woman who provocatively seems to strip as readers flip from the first cover to the second cover. (She doesn't really, of course.) Inside was a series of stories urging business leaders to consider becoming "See-Through CEOs". Clearly, the *Wired* editors assumed that readers would utter a collective: What!?! Because the very next section in this series of stories was a case study designed to prove this controversial point about transparency. *Wired* reported on real estate broker Glenn Kelman, CEO of a company called Redfin that was flailing around with a provocative marketing strategy—until Kelman took the daring step of deciding to admit to the world that his company's strategy had left his employees and customers—well, flailing around! In other words, he came clean. He shed all PR spin. He yanked the veneer off his firm. He stripped himself and his firm buck naked—and he saved his company. *Wired* concludes Kelman's story this way: "'Follow me,' he urged. And many have."

No kidding! That's actually what the *Wired* cover story said— as if this spiritual insight is big news in our day. Imagine that! For those of us on this Lenten journey, we say simply:

Follow us.

The Timeless Mystery of the Fourth Table

He is the image of the invisible God, the firstborn of all creation: for by him were all things created that are in Heaven and that are in the Earth—visible and invisible, whether they are thrones or dominions or principalities or powers. All things were created by him and for him. And he is before all things, and in him all things connect. And he is the head of the body, the church. He is the beginning, the firstborn from the dead; that in all things he might have preeminence. For it pleased the Father that in him should be the fullness of creation. And having made peace through the blood of his cross—by him, to reconcile all things unto himself, whether they be things on Earth or in Heaven.

—From Colossians 1:15-20

WHERE IN OUR STORY do you find salvation? We've raised this question before in our journey, because the answer isn't as easy as it seems. As Christians, we all know how to boil down the Good News into a couple of sentences. But, what we're saying here as the curtain falls on Act III of our four-act, five-table Lenten drama is this:

Beyond the first couple of sentences about salvation that most of us can recite by heart, what is the fullness of our faith? Or, let's put it another way: None of the four Gospels is two-sentences short! We've spent weeks on our Lenten journey—and we've only scratched the surface of the final days of Jesus' life. What's the larger story that Jesus wants us to learn about God's unfolding creation? Let's start today by recalling the tables we've explored already: first, the table at Bethany when Jesus was surprised by a woman's literally overflowing response; then, the tables Jesus overturned in the courtyards of the Temple as disturbing examples of community gone awry; then, the new kind of table Jesus established in his Last Supper with his disciples.

So, what's this fourth table? Well, we suggest today that the cross itself is a table. If you think this metaphor sounds odd, consider for a moment the ancient Orthodox customs on Holy Friday. If you've never experienced that liturgy in an Orthodox church, you might want to pay a visit this year. What you'll find on Holy Friday in Orthodox churches is a special, large cross on which the body of Jesus hangs crucified, sometimes in a life-sized iconic sculpture. Then, as the Holy Friday liturgy unfolds, the priest solemnly and lovingly approaches the cross, takes down the body of Jesus and carries it past the many icons that are arrayed across the front of the church—to lay Jesus' body on the altar table. These are the steps that lead toward the procession of Jesus' shroud, the *Epitaphios*, around the entire church. The shroud usually is an ornate fabric, decorated with a painted or embroidered icon of Jesus; and after the procession, the shroud is laid in a flower-bedecked wooden tomb that stands at the front of the church until the beginning of *Pascha*, or Easter.

In the West, we've lost most of that amazing imagery and movement that still dominates Orthodox life. We've lost our collective memory of such processions and such tangible use of sacred symbols. But—think about Jesus' crucified body literally juxtaposed with the table in this Eastern liturgy.

Puzzling over this imagery? Well, take a moment and re-read that dense, abstract language from the first chapter of Colossians and ponder the line: "In him, all things connect." Some translations render this closer to: "In him, all things hold together." Think of Jesus' arms, stretched on the cross, but also transformed as arms reaching out as if "to reconcile to himself all things, whether on Earth or in Heaven." The cross truly is shame, pain, sorrow and humiliation. It is violence, injustice and oppression. But the Christian story is about transformation—as we'll certainly see in the fourth and final act of our drama.

Think back through Jesus' life. What's Jesus' chemistry of community? It's the table—the custom of drawing all people around him into a circle that shares, learns, serves and eats together! So many of the greatest lessons of Jesus' life, if we think through the scope of his whole ministry, are associated with customs of eating and, thus, metaphors of a shared table. And now, the cross is no longer a call to wallow in suffering and gore, to glory in a primeval ritual of blood sacrifice. The cross is transformed into a sign of new hope. That rumbling we're feeling beneath our feet is not earth shattering. It's the creation renewing! As it says in Colossians: Not to destroy, but "to reconcile to himself all things."

All!

Now, that's a moment of truth that surely should knock us to our knees as Christians, isn't it? The Rev. Rob Bell, the best-selling evangelist who touched off a firestorm in 2011 with his teachings about an expansive Christian view of heaven, argues that this is a crucial truth in our faith. We don't invite people to the table, as Christians, because it's a nice or noble thing to do. No! Bell says we must invite all to the table, because God's creation—the larger kingdom to which Jesus is calling us—depends on all of us being there. Our salvation depends on welcoming a circle around this new table that is unbroken.

Finding our salvation in this story? The curtain is just about to drop on Act III, so a little time for prayer and reflection on these overwhelming truths certainly is in order. Think waaaay back for a moment—waaaay back past the beginning of our little Lenten story to the Nativity narrative. When the truths emerging around Mary became almost overwhelming, what did she do? Luke tells us, "Mary treasured up all these things and pondered them in her heart." So, even if we can't quite wrap our minds and hearts around such reflections in a single day—then, let's at least "treasure up all these things and ponder them."

Just before we pull the cords that drop this Act III curtain, let's add one more reflection on today's central metaphor. We need to ask ourselves in the intermission between this Act III and Act IV: Where else do we find the table Jesus envisioned? Where else must we work to build and rebuild the table in each new generation and repeat the invitation that calls the circle to form around it?

A Rolling Stone and Emily Dickinson's Overcoat

At the end of the Sabbath, as the first day of the week dawned, Mary Magdalene and the other Mary came to see the sepulcher. And, behold, there was a great Earthquake. The angel of the Lord descended from Heaven, and came and rolled back the stone from the door, and sat upon it. His countenance was like lightning, and his raiment white as snow.

—Matthew from Chapter 28

A death-blow is a life-blow to some
Who, till they died, did not alive become;
Who, had they lived, had died, but when
They died, vitality begun.

—Emily Dickinson, from *The Poems of Emily Dickinson*, "Part Four: Time and Eternity"

AFTER 37 DAYS ON the road, it's time in this final act of our drama for a pop quiz! But, don't worry. There are only two questions: Have our eyes, ears, minds and hearts been opened? And, do you remember all the stones we've seen? In these final four chapters of *Our Lent*, we're about to encounter four of the most significant things in our pilgrimage, each one a timeless echo of spiritual wisdom. And today? Our final stone lands **KA-BLAMMM** in our path.

How well do you recall the earlier stones? Remember Chapter 5: "Even Stones Cry Out" in which we encountered Luke's amazing tale of the stones in the roadway as Jesus entered Jerusalem? Here's how Luke described the stones that day:

> Some of the Pharisees in the crowd said to him, "Tell your disciples to keep still." And He answered, "I tell you, if these were silent, the stones would cry out."

Remember Chapter 12: "Stones as Spiritual IEDs" in which we explored Jesus' warning that God's kingdom involves unavoidable foundation stones. And, as Matthew put it:

> Anyone who falls on this stone shall be broken; but the person on whom the stone falls will be crushed into powder.

Remember Chapter 21: "Tumbling Milestones" in which Jesus warned that cycles of human creation and destruction are timeless truths that our faith must transcend. He pointed to the immense stones of the Jerusalem Temple and, Matthew reports, he said:

> Truly I say to you: There will not be left here one stone upon another; they all shall be thrown down.

On Easter morning, God demonstrates once and for all who is master of the stones. We especially like the Cecil B. DeMille details in Matthew's account of this—the earthquake and special lighting effects—which are lacking in the more bare-bones

Easter-morning narratives in the other Gospels. Surely, one of the greatest lines in all of world literature is: "His countenance was like lightning, and his raiment white as snow."

One level on which Christians celebrate this story each year focuses on what's inside the tomb: Nothing. That's a powerful, 2,000-year-old tradition that's central to Christianity. But, what we're saying today in our journey is this: Let's not forget the lesson of the moving stone itself. Jesus warned us that the stones would shout out—that the very foundation stones of our world would rock and rumble until our basic perceptions are shaken. And, now, we know—He was right!

It's so easy to miss this point in the midst of the earthquake and flashing lights: All along, Jesus was offering us a glimpse of the new kingdom he was calling us to help him re-create in this world. Our biggest challenge, he said—again and again—is opening our eyes, our ears, our hearts and our minds to discover this larger vision. Remember that day Jesus grabbed a fistful of budding fig branches and waved them in our faces—commanding us to simply: *look!*

Jesus is calling us to see these larger visions of our world—to help conquer the selfish and deadly powers of this world that seem to hem us into patterns of living that threaten to destroy us. But, no, Jesus doesn't appear in Act IV of the Gospels with any kind of healing medicine in his outstretched hand. In fact, in John's Chapter 20, the risen Christ responds to Thomas' doubts by inviting him to "reach out your finger, and behold my hands; and reach out your hand, and thrust it into my side." What Thomas discovers in this jarring scene is the revelation that Christians recall in art, in scripture and in preaching to this day: Even the risen Christ carries *wounds!*

A Public Broadcasting Service documentary, "Operation Homecoming," features the Vietnam veteran and author Tim O'Brien, who first popularized the phrase, *The Things They Carried*—a title to which we're paying respectful homage in our own Lenten title. O'Brien's 1990 novel recounted the powerful lessons he learned on battlefields in Vietnam, focusing readers on a whole series of things that GIs carried with them into battle from the basic emotions they carried within them to specific items of equipment—and even the candy in their pockets. Now, many years later, O'Brien appears in the PBS documentary, talking about the lives of GIs in Iraq. The main conclusion he draws from his own experience with wartime trauma is this: Healing from trauma isn't necessarily a healthy goal. After such deep trauma, we may never be able to heal. The healthier goal, he argues, is learning to live with the wounds we always will carry. This seems to be the path down which Jesus himself is leading us and is the subtitle of this book you are reading, as well.

After our weeks together, perhaps you are making these difficult connections, as well. In the final four scenes of this Lenten drama, we find Jesus underlining these spiritual insights. More than checking the tomb to see that it's empty, the point is to recall the rocking and rolling stone, remember who is master of the very stones and envision what kind of creation we are called to help restore—along with signs of the permanent injuries that we bear with us.

Are you familiar with Emily Dickinson's story? She was a recluse until her death at age 55 in 1886, privately writing nearly 2,000 poems that often reflected on intense matters of life and death. Yet, only a handful of her poems found their way into print during her lifetime. It wasn't until long after her death, through the influence of other writers like poet Conrad Aiken in the 1920s, that her work was widely read and finally earned the universal respect of literary scholars. To this day, scholars hotly contest details of her secretive life. How much did she suffer from illness, from unfulfilled romance, from religious controversy? Whatever the final scholarly verdicts on these issues, the truth is that, throughout her life, she somehow seemed unable to move from beyond the stony walls she had built around herself. And yet, she wrote those nearly 2,000 poems—each one, by its very definition, an act of faith in transcendence. Throughout her poetry, as we read it today, she carries both her private wounds and her irrepressible hope in life-transforming truths. Just read her nearly endless stream of poetry on the nature of death—and life—and you'll glimpse a scarred soul hoping to survive and emerge from the stones all around her. History's verdict says: She did! So, let's close with a benediction from Emily:

Death is a Dialogue between
The Spirit and the Dust.
"Dissolve" says Death—The Spirit "Sir
I have another Trust"—
Death doubts it—Argues from the Ground—
The Spirit turns away
Just laying off for evidence
An Overcoat of Clay.

Heartburn from the Stranger Dead Ahead

U.S. ARMY STAFF SGT. Jack Lewis, at age 40 with years of military service under his belt, thought he had seen everything the world could throw up into his path. As a young father, he had even suffered the tragic death of one of his infant daughters, who stopped breathing while she took a nap one day. He'd also served as a firefighter for a couple of years.

"So I had seen some bloody messes in my time and I had been in combat zones before where bad things happen," Lewis told me via telephone from the motorcycle shop where he was working in Seattle, Washington. "But what happened that night on that road in Iraq was something that I just couldn't mentally off-load after it happened. Eventually, I had to put it somewhere, so—one night after it happened, after I'd finished all my reports for the day, I just banged the story into my laptop and I emailed it to my blast-list of people who are special to me, who I needed to keep in the loop of my life.

"Telling that story was a way of saying I'm OK. It was a way of feeling that I was reconnecting with the real world. It was a way of asserting that I was still alive. It was a way of putting that story somewhere."

The story, called "Road Work," was discovered by PBS documentary filmmakers, through a program funded by the National Endowment of the Arts to collect and publish narratives written by U.S. troops serving in Iraq and Afghanistan. The moment the PBS filmmakers spotted Lewis' story, they knew where to put it: on national television. Their version of "Road Work", narrated by Lewis' own voice, was included in an hour-long film, *Operation Homecoming*. The visual images seared into Lewis' memory that night in Iraq were recreated by a remarkable crew of film technicians to bring Lewis' real life piece of short nonfiction vividly to life for the whole world to experience. Quite literally, "Road Work" is a contemporary gospel about this same thing we are encountering today in the final act of our Lenten journey: The unexpected stranger in our path.

Two thousand years ago, Jesus' followers learned a lot about strangers from Jesus himself before his execution by the Romans. As we approach the final passages in the Gospels, today, millions of Christians recall what happened next on the road to Emmaus: In the days after the crucifixion, the resurrected Jesus appeared and talked with two of his followers as they all walked along together. Even the phrase "Road to Emmaus" summons the ancient story. That phrase now is the title of paintings, etchings and sculptures. Psychologists, including Carl Jung, have pondered the meaning of this transformative scene. Despite all of that attention, the scene has nearly lost its power to shock us. But then, Jack Lewis thought he knew a lot about such things, himself, and he was unexpectedly knocked out of his boots on a dark roadway in Iraq one night by a completely unexpected, transformative encounter.

Here's how Luke tells the story in Chapter 24: Two of Jesus' followers, one named Cleopas and the other one never identified by Luke, are going to a village called Emmaus about seven miles from Jerusalem. They are talking with each other about all of the dramatic events that have unfolded. Then, a stranger suddenly looms in the roadway—so close that he falls in step with them. Luke tells us, as readers of the story, that this is Jesus—but Luke explains that Cleopas and his buddy have no idea who they are encountering!

Jesus even tries to jog some awareness by joining their conversation. Jesus asks them the equivalent of: "Hey, what's new?" But, Luke tells us that Cleopas and his buddy are so clueless—and so deep in mourning over the tragic events in Jerusalem—that they begin to rebuke the stranger in a rude manner. They frown and tell the stranger: "Are you the only stranger in Jerusalem who doesn't know what has just happened?"

This stranger refuses to simply reveal himself. Instead, Jesus eggs them on. He asks them, "What thing?"

Goaded in this way, Cleopas and his friend spend four whole verses of Luke spilling out the dramatic story of Jesus' life, death and the skeptical, confusing early reports about the empty tomb.

That's when Jesus lets them have it, although he still does not reveal his identity to these clueless clods. Jesus snaps at them: "Oh, fools! You're so slow of heart in believing all that the prophets have spoken!" Then, he goes on at length, essentially reading them the riot act about their skepticism and their overall lack of spiritual awareness. And they still don't recognize him!

Finally, they reach Emmaus and—at long last—they do the right thing and compassionately invite the stranger to stay with them and share an evening meal. While this stranger is picking up some bread, blessing it, breaking it, and passing it around the table—suddenly their eyes are opened and they recognize Jesus. At that point, their moment with Jesus is virtually over. He's gone from them in an instant! And all they are left with is the realization that "our hearts were burning within us while he talked with us along the road." Only at that point—as Jesus already has departed—do they realize that they should have recognized him along the road due to the sheer spiritual power of that connection they were feeling with this stranger. They would think about their encounter in the roadway the rest of their lives.

Jack Lewis said something like that about his year in Iraq and especially his encounter on a dark roadway one night. "This may sound like a glib answer, but I don't think it is: I'm going to be spending the rest of my life trying to figure out what happened to me in that year in Iraq." In "Road Work", he tells the story of a night patrol in which he and his men were traveling in complete darkness in an enormous, heavily armored, tank-like vehicle called a Stryker—except that night their Stryker struck a little Iraqi family car with an impact that flipped the Iraqi car and crushed its interior into what Lewis calls "a bloody mess." Climbing out of the Stryker to assess what had happened, Lewis was nearly deafened by the screaming of an old man who had survived the fearsome crash. He asked a translator to explain the old man's agonized cries. What he learned was that the remains of a young man inside the twisted car were this man's son—an honors student in engineering.

Having clearly conveyed that message, the old man continued to scream in Arabic.

Turning to the translator, Lewis asked: "What's he saying now?"

The translator's response: "He says to kill him, too."

As Lewis tells the story, he realized that this particular death of the boy in the car—among so many deaths unfolding in Iraq—was devastating because, without any warning in the midst of a close-to-ordinary evening in Iraq, "a monster had killed this man's son." The death of Lewis' daughter years before had not been nearly as violent as this man's loss of a son, but Lewis understood the spiritual devastation of losing a child. In that instant, "I knew how that one Iraqi man felt." In that instant, Lewis also realized, "He is not different from me."

Lewis had traveled half way around the world, carefully trained for all kinds of situations he might face in a war zone. But he wasn't trained—he couldn't have prepared at all—for this. In a lonely roadway, thousands of miles from home, he had suddenly jumped an even greater spiritual distance than he had traveled physically to reach Iraq. He had discovered himself—a father still mourning his own family's loss back home in America—mirrored in an unexpected stranger's form half a world away. The encounter changed Lewis' life forever.

So it was for Lewis—and, perhaps, so it can be for rest of us as we encounter strangers in our journeys. That's if we look carefully with compassionate, discerning eyes. Sometimes, a mysterious stranger on a lonely road can change our lives.

Exquisite Taste Around the Fifth Table!

DO YOU ENJOY THE natural world? Have you ever spent the night outdoors and then shaken off the damp, the aches and the chills to approach a breakfast fire—or, at least, experienced this through novels by authors like Larry McMurtry or Ernest Hemingway? If you're nodding your head to these questions, then you'll agree that the most exquisite post-resurrection scene in the Bible is Jesus beckoning his old friends to breakfast on the shore at dawn.

Remember, this is the setting in which Peter recognizes Jesus from the boat, pulls a fisherman's cloak around him and leaps into the water to reach Jesus first. Then, the others come to shore in their boat. At this point, here's how John sets this fifth and final table in our Lenten pilgrimage:

> As soon as they came to land, they saw a fire
> of coals there, and fish laid upon it, and bread.
> Jesus said to them: "Bring some of the fish that
> you have caught."

Note that detail? Jesus already has the fire burning and he's got a first helping of fish already sizzling there—but, he knows the taste of fresh-caught fish and he wants the men to bring some of that fresh-off-the-boat fish to share in the little circle he's forming on the shore. John continues, explaining that Peter quickly began unloading fish. And Jesus said to them, "Come and eat."

Somewhat nervously, they came. And John says: Jesus came and took the bread and gave it to them, and he did likewise with the fish. Do you see the pattern? An invitation. A circle forms. There's sustenance and there's sharing.

More than a decade ago, South African Archbishop Desmond Tutu visited Detroit and the mayor's office made a point of dispatching a plain-clothes detail of police to guard this world-famous civil rights hero. On Sunday morning, which oddly enough was the only down time left in the archbishop's busy schedule, he invited me to interview him in his suite at the Renaissance Center hotel. We had met a few times over the years and he graciously made arrangements to spend an unhurried hour answering questions on this occasion.

However, after I trekked all the way into the downtown area, parked and made my way up to Tutu's suite, the archbishop came to the door of his room with a worried frown. "There has been a change," he said. "No interview now, I am sorry to tell you. I must use this hour for something more pressing."

As I stood in the hallway, peering into his sitting room through the open door, several tall men in dark suits were visible as they sat rather awkwardly in easy chairs.

"Anything serious?" I asked, wanting an explanation but not wanting to be rude.

"Well, it was a discovery I made just a little while ago, or I would have telephoned you not to drive down here," he said. "It seems that every single man in my police detail here either sings in a choir or is a deacon in his church—and I am the cause preventing these four fine men from serving in their parishes today. I cannot ignore this situation."

"What do you plan to do?" I inquired.

"Well, we have ordered some wine and a loaf of bread from room service and—of course—we must hold a liturgy here," he said. "It will take me an hour, I should think."

I stood silently for a long moment.

"Are you a man of faith?" he asked at length. "Would you like to join us for our little Eucharist?"

What do you think happened next? Who could refuse such an invitation? This is why one of the most memorable tables in my own life is an ordinary glass-topped, chrome-framed coffee table in a hotel sitting room in Detroit—because, around that table, Tutu invited five of us to join him as he prayed, taught, chanted a Psalm and finally consecrated bread and wine to share with us.

As I read about that scene on the shoreline in the middle of John 21, I can feel the electricity those men felt that morning. Just as the five of us were in Tutu's hotel suite as he celebrated the Eucharist just for us—Jesus' followers on that shoreline 2,000 years ago surely were walking on pins and needles as they approached the breakfast fire. What was happening? Who was this? They were virtually certain it was Jesus, but none of them "dared to ask," John writes. The connections in this spiritual journey often are extremely difficult to discern. But, Jesus kept pointing, time and time again, to this symbol—this thing—that is so central to the kingdom he sees emerging: a table. Remember the pattern: An invitation. A circle forms. There's sustenance and there's sharing.

Are you still a little nervous as we approach this next-to-the-last thing in our 40-part journey? Are you a little unclear, still, about how broadly we should think about this critically important thing—this fifth table that Jesus is laying out for us?

In truth, it's not nearly as hard as it may seem. In our adventure, we've already encountered the depths of Robert Frost's poetic vision. If you missed that chapter, go back and check it out—because there's some unforgettable imagery in that Chapter 22 on the poetry of war. These things all have a way of becoming inextricable tiles in the mosaic of our lives.

Forty years ago, the first Robert Frost poem that I ever memorized was so simple that it barely seemed like poetry at all. But the lines wear so well through the many ages in a person's life that it's the one poem that prefaces most collections of Frost's poetry to this day. It's a simple hymn about the gathering of two people in a rural setting—and it goes like this:

> *I'm going out to clean the pasture spring;*
> *I'll only stop to rake the leaves away*
> *(And wait to watch the water clear, I may):*
> *I shan't be gone long.—You come too.*
> *I'm going out to fetch the little calf*
> *That's standing by the mother. It's so young,*
> *It totters when she licks it with her tongue.*
> *I shan't be gone long.—You come too.*

In much the same way, the invitation went out from the little fire along the shore in Galilee 2,000 years ago, the tangy smoke tickling our nostrils and the warmth soothing our damp and aching bones. Who could resist such an exquisitely delicious invitation?

Oddly enough, so many of us do resist, don't we? Perhaps we're urgently headed somewhere else on such a busy morning. Perhaps we don't have time for this—period! But that fire still is burning on a shoreline near us. And the invitation echoes through all times and places:

We shan't be long. You come too.

Carrying Stories to Fill the Whole World

WHAT'S LEFT? WE'VE ALREADY enjoyed the most exquisite breakfast we've ever tasted and now the rising sun is at our backs as we return to the rest of our lives. Plus, it's a holiday season! We're just about to enjoy Easter dinner with our families and, then—then, we seriously need a good long nap. So, haven't we covered everything already?

Not quite! There's one last thing, hanging there like one of those antique ribbon bookmarks from the final page of the final Gospel—that is, if we can remember what's there in those final verses of John's 21st chapter. Can you recall?

It's books. Lots and lots of books. Don't feel bad if this image didn't immediately leap to the front of your mind. I haven't met a single person in the many months it took to prepare this 40-day reflection who could recall immediately what was contained in the final verses of the final Gospel. Remember that John's Gospel opens with:

> In the beginning was the Word, and the Word
> was with God, and the Word was God.

Then 21 chapters later, John closes with lines that include, in most translations, a very curious word: "If." The final passage goes like this:

> There are also many other things that Jesus did. If every one of them were written down, I suppose that even the world itself could not contain the books that would be written.

Translations vary, but the vast majority—including Eugene Peterson's contemporary paraphrase, "The Message"—position that little word "if" right in the middle of John 21:25. How strange of John to finish his truly grand opera of a Gospel in this odd, folksy voice of a storyteller. The style of this line feels more like J.R.R. Tolkien or C.S. Lewis than the author of a Gospel. Remember that John is famous as the Gospel writer who casts his scenes in such clear-cut, black-and-white terms: What about Judas? He was a demon! Who carried Jesus' cross? Jesus carried it alone! And so on. John does not quibble or encourage speculation. Then, this oddly fuzzy little tag is left hanging off the end of his Gospel—the very definition of a loose end.

Even though our *Things We Carry* narrative now has run into 40 chapters (not a concise 21 like John's Gospel)—we know what John is talking about when he says that there's never enough space to exhaust our story. There were a lot more things we could have written about in our meditations. We never explored things like the crown of thorns, for instance, or the nature of the rooms—from poor homes to imperial halls—through which Jesus passes. In the chapters we have shared with you, lots of details were left on the cutting-room floor, mostly for reasons of clarity and focus.

But, here's a good example of a gem that was lost in the cutting—and that now sparkles back at us in the context of this final chapter—our final moments together in this Lenten season. Remember Chapter 22 about poetry and war's rumors, featuring a story about Russian poet Joseph Brodsky? In that chapter, I described how the poet fled the Soviet Union and, in the mid 1970s, wound up at the University of Michigan in Ann Arbor, where he was supposed to teach poetry and immediately collided with his first class of university students. I say "collided" because Brodsky came to the seminar room with a far greater urgency about the nature of poetry than those shaggy-haired, up-scale American kids could begin to imagine. It's true that, as the discussion unfolded in Brodsky's first session with the young skeptics who had enrolled in his class, these kids had no inkling of this poet's global stature. More than a decade later, in 1987, he would win the Nobel Prize for Literature. It's also true—just as we reported in Chapter 22—that Brodsky finally did have to explain to these privileged university students that words weren't merely intellectual toys.

His line, which his students would never forget, was: "If you are sent to a prison camp — the poetry you carry in your memory may be your entire world. So, we must choose well what world we will carry, no?" However, one detail we didn't include in Chapter 22, was that it was me—your guide through *Our Lent: Things We Carry*—who finally, after a long discussion with Brodsky, managed to recite the first Psalm of the evening: Psalm 90. That night, Psalm 90 was recited from the King James Version that includes the memorable verses:

> We spend our years as a tale that is told. … So
> teach us to number our days, that we may apply
> our hearts unto wisdom.

More than 30 years later, I still recall Brodsky, looking out a window, smoking quietly and nodding his head in the cadence of Psalm 90 as it resonated in the Residential College seminar room in Ann Arbor. What were his associations with Psalm 90 that evening? I had no clue as I recited and he nodded thoughtfully. Years later, after reading Brodsky's books and, then, a couple of biographies of the poet, I envisioned him perhaps reciting those lines to himself at various points in his own life. Perhaps he mumbled the words to himself in Russian after he was sentenced by the Soviet court for defying the state's official policies for poets—and found himself rattling along inside a prison train bound for God only knew where. I do know one truth, though: Across the immense difference in our life experiences, somehow we connected in that shared Psalm on that one evening.

The idea that our spiritual calling involves sharing our stories with one another isn't something that's universally celebrated in Christian teaching. There have been long periods and powerful movements in Christian mysticism, over the centuries, that have argued for a spiritual goal of completely submerging our individual lives, hearts and spirits in the body of Christ—to such an extreme degree that we humbly deny any value as individuals. People talk about "crushing" or even "annihilating" ourselves as individual personalities in our pursuit of mystic union. Many writers and preachers have encouraged others to go and do likewise.

Such voices still echo. The French philosopher turned Christian mystic, Simone Weil, whose writings has seen something of a revival in the last couple of decades, wrote to a friend in 1942: "Nothing concerning me can have any kind of importance." It's part of a long passage in which she talks about the "valueless" nature of her individual life. However, if—and this is another enormous "if" like the one that closes John's Gospel—if Weil's writings had not survived her death at age 34 of tuberculosis in 1943, the world would have been a poorer place. Her story, although often austere and extreme in its observations, is a powerful gospel in itself. The heroic example of her life, including her commitment to the French Resistance in World War II, and the challenging spiritual ideas she continues to spread throughout the world via her surviving writings, have prompted many people to suggest that she is an ideal saint for our times. Clearly, by the way she lived and wrote, she transcended her own 1942 argument that seemed to declare her own life as unexceptional, unimportant and valueless.

There's proof of this spiritual principle in the works of writers as diverse as Charles Dickens and Jane Austen, Jack Kerouac and C.S. Lewis, Gabriel Garcia Marquez and Joan Didion. This is why J.R.R. Tolkien ends his *Lord of the Rings* trilogy with Frodo handing over to his friend Sam the priceless "big book with plain red leather covers" in which he and Bilbo already have filled nearly

80 chapters of the narrative. The story is precious, both because it was experienced at a dire cost in human life and because the narrative the book contains is timeless. Yet, Frodo does not fill the entire book. He intentionally leaves some blank pages at the end and, as he gives the book to his dear friend Sam, he says, "The last pages are for you."

This is what John is saying in the closing of his Gospel: Not that the story is finished—but that John is finished writing. He is saying, in effect: The ultimate thing in our human pilgrimage through God's creation is the story itself—the narrative we carry with us into the rest of the world that can connect and reconcile all things.

So it was shared 2,000 years ago in the last of the last of the Gospels. The message is timeless and true: Our salvation is inextricably bound up with those things we choose to carry with us as we move through the world. And, the most important thing of all that we bear is the story we have been given to share.

About the Author

DAVID CRUMM IS BEST known as a journalist for more than 30 years, specializing in reporting on the impact of faith and culture on people's daily lives. Beginning in the early 1980s, he reported across the U.S. and occasionally from other parts of the world for the Detroit Free Press and its wire services. In 2006, his weekly column on everyday spirituality won the annual Wilbur Award for "Best Column on Religion in a Major Newspaper." That was his sixth Wilbur award, among many honors over the years. In 2007, Crumm left the Free Press to found David Crumm Media LLC and ReadTheSpirit publishing. In partnership with software developer John Hile, who serves as publisher of the new venture—and in cooperation with media professionals from across the U.S.—Crumm and Hile launched the www.ReadTheSpirit.com online magazine and related publishing projects. The entire team produces media from daily articles to complete books and small-group resources exploring religion, spirituality, values and cultural competency. ReadTheSpirit's guiding principle is: Making spiritual connections for everyday living.

Colophon

READ THE SPIRIT BOOKS produces its titles using innovative digital systems that serve the emerging wave of readers who want their books delivered in a wide range of formats—from traditional print to digital readers in many shapes and sizes. This book was produced using this entirely digital process that separates the core content of the book from details of final presentation, a process that increases the flexibility and accessibility of the book's text and images. At the same time, our system ensures a well-designed, easy-to-read experience on all reading platforms, built into the digital data file itself.

David Crumm Media has built a unique production workflow employing a number of XML (Extensible Markup Language) technologies. This workflow, allows us to create a single digital "book" data file that can be delivered quickly in all formats from traditionally bound print-on-paper to nearly any digital reader you care to choose, including Amazon Kindle®, Apple iBook®, Barnes and Noble Nook® and other devices.

Due to the highly adaptable "print-on-demand" process we use for printed books, we invite you to visit us online to learn more about opportunities to order quantities of this book with the possibility of personalizing a "group read" for your organization or congregation. A personalized "group read" can include a specially customized shipment of books to you with your group's logo and name on the covers of books you order. You can even add your own introductory pages to these customized books for your church or organization. Visit us online for more details or to see examples of what other groups have created.

During production, we use Adobe InDesign®, <Oxygen/>® XML Editor and Microsoft Word® along with custom tools built in-house.

The print edition is set in Myriad Pro and Minion Pro.

Cover art and Design by Rick Nease: www.RickNeaseArt.com.

Copy editing and XML styling by Celeste Dykas.

Digital encoding and print layout by John Hile.?

If you enjoyed this book, you may also enjoy

Glitter in the Sun explores how we can glimpse truths of our faith through the Twilight saga. These tales remind us of the eternal power of Love. The Bible tells us that ultimately only God can love us in a truly timeless way.

http://www.JamesBondBibleStudy.com

ISBN: 978-1-934879-40-5

If you enjoyed this book, you may also enjoy

Here's a book that will reward your efforts as you look at evil through the eyes of Ian Fleming's James Bond. Like Bond, you too might be roused to take on the dragons of evil in our midst.

http://www.JamesBondBibleStudy.com

ISBN: 978-1-934879-11-5

If you enjoyed this book, you may also enjoy

In his new Guide for Grief, the Rev. Rodger Murchison brings years of pastoral experience and study, sharing recommendations from both scripture and the latest research into loss and bereavement.

http://www.GuideForGrief.com

ISBN: 978-1-934879-31-3

If you enjoyed this book, you may also enjoy

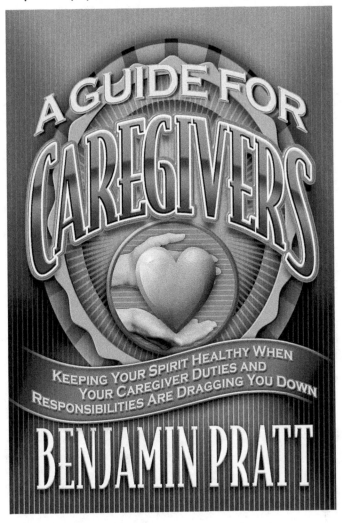

In one out of three households, someone is a caregiver: women and men who give of body, mind and soul to care for the well being of others. They need daily, practical help in reviving their spirits and avoiding burnout.

CPSIA information can be obtained
at www.ICGtesting.com
Printed in the USA
BVHW040300250419
546414BV00009B/143/P